Taking Your Business into Europe

Peter Walker

Published by Hawksmere Ltd
12–18 Grosvenor-Gardens
London
SW1W 0DH

British Library Cataloguing in
Publication Data
Walker, Peter
  Taking your business into Europe.
  1. Europe. Business firms. Organisation
  I. Title
  658.1'1'094

ISBN 1-85418-045-2
ISBN 1-85418-005-3 pbk

Printed in Great Britain by Biddles Ltd,
Guildford and King's Lynn

CONTENTS

Part 2

Practical considerations

Part 3

A case study – retailing

Part 4

Appendices

Acknowledgements

Many people have helped to make this book possible, and particular thanks are given to the following companies and organisations who have given both encouragement and information:

The Albion Trust Group of Companies

Barclays Bank plc

Computacenter Limited

Grundmann (UK) Limited

Institute of Financial Accountants

NFC Contract Distribution

Paragon Communications plc

Prime Computer Limited

The Sock Shop International plc

GLOSSARY

AFNOR • The French equivalent of the BSI

BC-NET • Business cooperation network – a pilot scheme set up by the Commission to give small and medium-sized businesses in Member States a network of contacts to help them expand

BSI • British Standards Institution responsible for standards in the UK

CEDEFOP • European Centre for the Development of Vocational Training

CEN • European Standardisation Committee

CENELEC • European Standardisation Committee for Electrical Products

The Commission • The civil service of the Community

The Common Market • see EEC

The Community • see EEC

COREPER • Committee of Permanent Representatives of Member States

The Council • A policy-making body of the Community

The Court of Auditors • Auditors of Community revenue and expenditure

DIN • The German equivalent of the BSI

DTI • Department of Trade and Industry

EAEC • European Atomic Energy Community

EAGGF Guidance • European Agricultural Guidance and Guarantee Fund

EC • European Community – see EEC

ECJ • European Court of Justice

ECGD • Export Credits Guarantee Department

Economic and Social Committee • Advisory body which must be consulted by the Commission on proposals relating to economic and social matters

ECSC • European Coal and Steel Community

ECU • European Currency Unit

EDF • European Development Fund

EEC • European Economic Community

EFTA • European Free Trade Association, whose members are Austria, Finland, Iceland, Norway, Sweden and Switzerland. It is regarded as a trading partner of the EEC

EIB • European Investment Bank

EMCF • European Monetary Cooperation Fund – this administers the EMS

EMS • European Monetary System

ERM • Exchange Rate Mechanism – this regulates exchange rates of those members belonging to the scheme. The UK, Greece, Spain and Portugal do not participate in it

ERDF • European Regional Development Fund

ESF • European Social Fund

EUREKA • A European institution aimed at encouraging R&D collaboration

European Commission • see Commission

European Community • see EEC

European Parliament • A body of elected representatives, who can amend, accept or reject (by an absolute majority) Council proposals

EUROSTAT • This is the statistical office of the Community

FEOGA Guidance • European Agricultural Guidance and Guarantee Fund

IMPS • Integrated Mediterranean Programmes

Lomé Convention • This is between the Community and sixty African, Caribbean and Pacific countries. The aim is to provide aid through the European Development Fund (EDF)

Member States • Countries belonging to the EEC, i.e. Belgium, France, Denmark, Germany (Federal Republic of, or West, Germany), Greece, Ireland, Italy, Luxembourg, The Netherlands, Portugal, Spain, and the United Kingdom

OJ • The Official Journal of the European Community, in which will be found EEC legislation and the like

PEDIP • Programme for modernisation of Portuguese industry

R&D • Research and development

SAD • The Single Administrative Document has replaced the many export and import documents once required by each Member State

SEA • Single European Act

Single European Act • An international treaty modifying the EEC Treaty and setting the deadline of 31 December 1992 for the establishment of the Single Market in Europe

PART 1
Business opportunities
The Single Market

CHAPTER 1
The Single Market opportunity

| 1.1 | **Europe without frontiers** |

Businesses now have an exciting opportunity to increase sales and profits. They must not miss it, because with the opportunity comes more competition and the danger that they could be driven out of business completely.

The reason is to be found in the establishment of what is known as the Single Market in Europe, which the European Commission describes as 'Europe without frontiers'. By 31 December 1992, in accordance with an international treaty called the Single European Act, it is planned to abolish the final barriers to trade within the twelve countries of the Common Market (or European Community).

This plan is not restricted to a reduction of the paperwork complications of sending goods abroad. Technical standards will be harmonised in order to make the specification and manufacture of products easier. National and local authorities will not be able to reject tenders for contracts from businesses based in countries outside their own. Companies and professional firms will find it easier to establish branches or new enterprises in other European Community Member States.

All this is good for business, because a company based in, say, the UK has access to more customers. Indeed, more people live in the Community than in the USA or the USSR. The full potential of this market is illustrated further in Appendix 1 of this book.

1.2	## Action – not just awareness

Businesses must be more than aware of what is happening. Lord Young, Secretary of State for Trade and Industry, pointed out (*DTI Single Market News* October 1988) that awareness 'counts for very little unless business really gets to grip with the implications of the fundamental changes taking place in the Community's trading rules'.

He added, 'What matters at the end of the day, though, is not awareness or even understanding, but action: action by every firm in the country.' The first stage in such action involves planning, and the initial steps are high-lighted in chapter 2. Subsequent chapters of this book illustrate how the plan or strategy can be made into reality, but the time to prepare is now.

It is not easy, but a lot of help is available. Useful names and addresses are listed in Appendix 3, while solutions to the all-important problem of raising finance are noted in chapter 10. Awareness can therefore be turned into action, because businesses can be guided to take advantage of the Single Market in Europe.

1.3	## Failure to act – business disaster

Lord Young stressed both the positive and negative aspects of the Single Market. 'Europe is providing an increasingly important market for UK produced goods and the creation of the Single Market by the end of 1992 provides us all with both an opportunity and a challenge. It will give our exporters a home market of 320 million people for their goods but at the same time, open up our domestic market to EC imports.'

The message is quite clear. Although businesses based in the UK are being encouraged to take advantage of the enlarged market, governments in other Member States are in turn encouraging their nationals to do the same. The increased competition is coming to these shores. Bus-inesses which do nothing could be forced out altogether, because someone with a competitively priced product in, say, Milan has decided to sell it in the UK.

A conscious decision to concentrate in the home market is not necessarily a mistake. As explained in the next chapter, there can be good reasons for taking this view. It must, however, be a conscious decision in full knowledge of the competition as part of a business strategy. Those enterprises which decide on such a course must still keep an eye both on that competition, and on European developments in the field of standards as explained in chapter 7.

The effects of the Single Market in Europe will therefore be felt on domestic trade. This of course can be good news for importers, agents and distributors in the UK. Overseas businesses will be keen to use their services as pointed out in chapter 3. Increased competition from abroad is not going to be bad news for all enterprises.

1.4 | Remaining differences

The objective of completely harmonised rules for trade in the European Community by the end of 1992 will not be achieved. There will still be differences.

Some of these will arise out of the length of time needed to make the necessary technical changes. In the UK, for example, there is the square-pin electrical plug, but other countries insist on round pins, and frown upon the supply of electrical appliances not already fitted with them. Other such differences can be solved by industry itself, and examples of how this can be done will be found in chapter 7.

In addition to these technical variations there are differing legal practices, of which examples are noted in chapters 3 and 5. Achievements of the Community in the field of harmonisation will, on the other hand, be found in Appendix 2.

The most important difference of all, however, is people. Tastes, practices and, of course, languages are not the same throughout Europe. Businesses must find out what these are before they can effectively market their products or services in the Community. Chapter 3 contains some ideas as to how this can be done, while there are some pointers towards useful sources of information in Appendices 1, 3 and 4.

1.5 | More business – go for it!

The Single Market in Europe consequently provides opportunities for businesses wishing to start or expand their activities in various ways:

(1) by exporting (see chapters 1 and 3),

(2) by starting new branches or overseas companies (chapter 4),

(3) by acquiring, taking over or merging with another enterprise either in the UK to establish a strong home base, or in another country (chapter 3),

(4) by increasing their home market with new products from other Member States (chapter 3).

Businesses from outside the Common Market should consider the benefits of setting up a factory in the UK as a base for expansion into the Community. Provided that they use mostly EC-made components, their products may be regarded as emanating from the Community, and exempt from customs duties.

Whether or not any of these is the right approach will be decided by the essential strategic plan (chapter 2). In this context Sir Denys Henderson, Chairman of ICI, drew the right conclusion in the October 1988 *DTI Single Market News*. 'We in Europe are slipping in the industrial world league table. Now we have a marvellous chance to lift our commercial horizons and build our competitive strength for the 1990s and beyond. Let's go for it!'

CHAPTER 2
A strategy for business expansion

2.1	**Introduction**

The Single Market of the Community will result in greater competition and more opportunities for businesses in the UK, so they will need a strategy either to handle the former or to take advantage of the latter. It must, however, not be ignored. There are many examples of British businesses which have failed to take notice of overseas competition, and which have suffered as a result. There are no longer lots of British motorbikes on the roads, while John Owens, Deputy Director General of the Confederation of British Industry, warned in January 1989, 'Nearly ten thousand UK companies are sleepwalking towards 1992. Many of them will go out of business in the early 'nineties, unless they start preparing now for the complete abolition of trade barriers within the European Community in less than four years' time.'

It is therefore essential to compile a strategic plan appropriate for the situation, and not be one of the four in five firms which, according to a CBI survey, were failing to take such action. The same principles for a plan of this kind apply to all businesses whatever their size, although the strategy for a small enterprise will obviously be less complicated than for a multi-national.

A plan need not be rigid – some companies pride themselves on their ability to react quickly to changing situations. This can be achieved by, say, a small sales marketing and creative team, while the prompt reaction is achieved through subcontracting the production of the final article. The business therefore does not have to invest in expensive equipment, yet can achieve good results. Such an enterprise still needs to plan its strategy for the future.

This chapter therefore contains the main points to be considered in compiling the plan and putting it into practice. The process consists of:

(1) obtaining information about the market and competitors,

(2) analysing the business's existing resources and potential for expansion,

(3) making policy decisions,

(4) working out how the plan is to be implemented,

(5) monitoring progress.

Many businesses have appointed a director or key manager who is to coordinate their European activities. He or she will therefore play the leading role in the strategic plan although will, of course, be assisted by the appropriate personnel at each stage.

2.2 | Marketing – a check list

(1) Know the competition – this is both a defensive and offensive requirement. Such knowledge can help in identifying areas of expansion or of trouble. Important factors to be found out about competitors include product quality, price, locations, marketing policies (e.g. selling methods, outlets), after-sales service, size of competitor, market segment (e.g. lower priced or quality goods, percentage of the market), financial information, their respective strengths and weaknesses, and their plans as revealed by, for example, the press, computer data bases or specialist books containing appropriate analyses.

(2) Know the potential customers – the purpose is to identify needs, so that the business can fulfil them, perhaps by changing the existing products. If the

business sells to distributors, then it must also understand the needs of the ultimate consumers. Market research of some kind should be considered, but the use of agencies may be too expensive. If, however, the plan is merely to sell to distributors, then these are the people who will know the market, and can advise accordingly.

(3) Economic considerations include those such as inflation, movements of population and the other matters mentioned particularly in Appendix 1.

2.3 Self-examination

As part of establishing a strategy a business must question its own activities with the objective of becoming more efficient and capable of expansion. This is what is known as the company or business audit. Key areas include:

(1) Can the company operate more effectively by investing in new technology or by developing more low-cost processes or designs?

(2) Is the business in the right location to take advantage of any expansion?

(3) Should the company reduce or expand its product range or services, or should it concentrate on one area of the market?

(4) Should the business change its products or services in the light of the market research findings?

(5) Are the products or services being distributed through the right channels?

(6) Can the products or services be made to stand out from those offered by the competition and in such a way as to fulfil a known need?

(7) Should there be more research and development?

(8) Can a product range be expanded to meet a perceived need by obtaining licensed technology or know-how?

(9) If market research reveals that competition is too severe, can the emphasis of the business be changed

into other areas or segments of the market less attractive to competitors?

(10) Can the business be increased by providing add-ons to the competitor's products?

(11) Can buying be done more efficiently or cheaply?

(12) Can the distribution system be improved?

(13) Should the existing PR and advertising methods be changed?

(14) What is the capacity of the existing business and how far can it cope with expansion?

(15) What personnel policies and training needs will result from any expansion?

(16) How will competitors react to any changes?

(17) What are the weaknesses and strengths of the business's management, marketing, product ranges, and distribution?

2.4 Policy for the Community

Once the market research and self-examination has been completed the next stage is to frame a policy for business expansion into the market. The aspects to be considered include:

(1) Should the expansion be by means of the establishment of an overseas subsidiary and, if so, should this be by means of a takeover, merger or acquisition?

(2) Should the business prepare itself for expansion into Europe by building up a stronger home base, by such means as a takeover, merger or acquisition of another company in the UK?

(3) Where should any subsidiary or branch be established? The answer to this question will usually require further research, and staff will often have to be sent overseas to survey local conditions before it can be answered.

(4) Should the expansion be through a joint venture?

(5) Should any increased business be as a result of the licensing of technology or know-how?

(6) Can any increased business be serviced entirely from the UK?

(7) Can business be increased through agents, distributors or franchises?

(8) Can any increased production needs be met by means of subcontracting?

(9) Will extra resources and cash be required?

(10) Can distributors or agents in the UK increase their range of products by obtaining agencies or distributorships from expanding businesses in the Community?

(11) Businesses based in countries outside the Community will have to question whether or not the UK (or any other Member State) is the right place in which to base their European activities.

2.5 The operations plan

Once the policy for expansion has been decided, the next stage is to work out how this is to be done. Points for consideration are:

(1) The professional team that may be required, particularly where the plan is to take over an overseas business or to open a subsidiary or branch in another Community country. Even where expansion is to be obtained through the appointment of an overseas distributor, a lawyer will have to be appointed to draw up the agreement. Note that some smaller firms of solicitors are unlikely to have the expertise to do this. The Law Society will have a list of firms with an indication of their particular specialisations.

(2) The compiling of a plan to be presented to a bank or investor in order to obtain sufficient funds. The answer as to whether or not the business expands into other Community countries will often depend on the availability of funds from such sources.

(3) The appointment of suitable overseas agents, distributors or other suitable sales staff.

(4) Changes in production, selling, marketing or other procedures or methods as a result of the policy decision. Quality control is particularly important.

(5) The products or services to be offered abroad.

(6) The registration of patents and trade marks overseas. This can be an expensive process, but is essential in the case of an innovative product. Where patents are concerned speed is essential. The general rule is that applications for registration should be made in the various countries at more or less the same time. There is now a European patent, but this is still a slow and expensive process, because the application has effectively to be processed in all the Community countries. In these circumstances a patent agent is an essential member of the professional team mentioned in (1) above. UK patent agents can help with the procedures both in this country and overseas.

(7) After-sales service and the possible appointment of local service agents.

(8) Staff training needs and policies towards employees in general. This must include the preparation of staff for cultural differences, and assistance, such as language classes, for those and their families who have to move overseas. People must also become aware of any relevant overseas or general standards. Where expansion results in the recruitment of employees abroad, then the public relations aspect in relation to those people must be considered.

(9) Advertising and public relations. Brochures, instruction books, packaging material and the like must all be reviewed and translated into appropriate languages.

(10) Administrative changes to cope with expansion. This should include any computing or communications needs.

(11) Changes in accountancy procedures. Accoun-

tants will have to cope with multi-currency accounts and currency management. Overseas operations will have to be monitored carefully.

(12) Credit control. It may be better to use the services of an agency with expertise in credit collection overseas. Factoring is another possibility.

(13) Sales and other forecasting relating to the business activities and needs.

(14) Property needs.

(15) Purchasing policy. Materials may have to be purchased from different or cheaper sources of supply.

(16) Transportation and warehousing.

(17) Research and development needs. As well as any specifically European R&D projects mentioned in chapter 7, local polytechnics or universities may be happy to collaborate on specific projects.

(18) Membership of appropriate organisations, such as Chambers of Commerce or the British Standards Institute, in order to take advantage of their advisory services and business contacts.

(19) Insurance needs of the expanded business.

Once the various aspects of the plan have been decided upon, they should be written down in a time scale. Because there are many components to it, it may be necessary to use techniques such as critical path analysis, to see how each part integrates with the others.

2.6 Monitoring the strategic plan

Once the operations plan is agreed it must be monitored in respect of two areas:

(1) the implementation of the plan itself,

(2) the follow-up to the plan such as the performance of the new overseas branch.

If there are many aspects to the strategy, the task of monitoring it may have to be given to various managers or employees. These would report to the director or senior executive ultimately responsible for ensuring that it all works.

The follow-up will be a continuing process, and can be a big job if the expansion has involved overseas branches, changes in production techniques, etc. One means of coordinating it is to appoint a Compliance Officer with the responsibility of ensuring that the plan is being followed. He or she would also have the task of seeing that EEC rules and regulations are complied with. The person for such a task would have to have a wide and practical background in the business. It is, however, useful for a company to have on the payroll some people who are not specialists, but who are sound generalists. They can bring together all aspects of the enterprise, because they understand how they work together.

The preparation of a business strategy is an essential part of success in expanding activities beyond national frontiers. Things will go wrong because no one can foresee everything, so businesses, their advisers and consultants must be flexible in their reactions to changing situations. Everyone must work together to plan for the effects of the Single Market in Europe on their clients' or their own enterprises.

CHAPTER 3
Increased sales
Agencies, distributorships, know-how and franchising

3.1	**Increased sales to other countries in Europe**

Many businesses will be wanting to expand by opening new markets for themselves in other countries but lack the resources to set up their own operations elsewhere. Indeed, prospective sales may be insufficient to justify such a major step.

The answers can be found in the appointment of agents, distributors or franchisees. Businesses with bright ideas but limited resources or objectives could gain valuable royalty income by licensing their know-how. Others will obtain extra income from franchising. It is of course important to consider these options carefully because of Community and differing national laws.

At the same time there will be opportunities for agencies, distributorships, and franchisees in the UK. Companies in other European Community countries are also looking for opportunities further afield as a result of the promotion of the 1992 idea.

3.2	**Agencies**

3.2.1 Definition of an agent

Before a decision is made on whether to appoint an agent, a business must know what is involved. As a first step a definition will be helpful, although not all experts are agreed as to what this should be.

According to G. H. L. Fridman the essence of agency

is that the agent has the power to affect his or her principal's legal relations with the outside world (*Law of Agency* 4th edition Butterworth 1976). For example, most agencies will require the agent to obtain orders, which the principal then will be under a legal duty to fulfil. Provided that the buyer knows that the goods or services are being purchased through an agency, if anything goes wrong it is the seller, not its agent, which is responsible.

The word 'agent' is sometimes used by business-people when they really mean 'distributor'. More information will be found in 3.3 below.

The relationship is therefore governed by a contract between the agent and the person or business making the appointment, although there are some other general legal rules. For example, in English law an agent is not allowed to make a secret profit out of the transactions made on behalf of the principal. A simple example is found in a case, *De Bussche v Alt* [1878] ChD 286, where a Japanese agent had been appointed to sell a ship. He could not find a buyer at the price so, without informing his principal, he bought it for himself. He later made a profit for himself by selling the ship at a much higher price, but the English High Court made him give this secret profit back to his principal.

Indeed the agent is normally expected to make his or her money from the commission paid by the principal on each sale. In this respect an agency can be an effective sales and credit control aid because many, if not most, contracts provide for such commission only to be paid after the customer has paid.

Such a term applies to the normal sales agency, but there are various types of agent of which examples are:

(1) A general agent who is given authority to do some act in the ordinary course of his or her business as an agency.

(2) A special agent who has limited authority to do particular actions or to represent the principal in a

particular transaction or series of transactions. A sales agent, for example, may be employed to obtain orders for a specific range of products.

(3) A factor or a 'mercantile agent' who in 'the customary course of his business' has 'authority to sell goods or to consign goods for the purposes of sale, or to raise money on the security of goods' – s 1 Factors Act 1889. A person who buys goods from a factor is not usually given the identity of their owner.

(4) A broker who represents a principal for negotiating purposes only. He or she is never given possession of any goods or documents of title.

(5) Del credere agents who are given extra commission, for which they will indemnify their principal if the customer fails to pay for the goods.

3.2.2 *Terms of an agent's appointment – a check list*

Although an agency agreement should be drafted by a lawyer, the prospective principal (or agent) for the purposes of negotiating the deal should have a check list of the points to be covered. They should include:

(1) the correct names and addresses of the parties – trading names are not enough,

(2) the territory in which the goods or services are to be sold,

(3) the procedure if enquiries are received from outside the territory,

(4) a description of the goods and services,

(5) details of any training to be provided for the agent,

(6) whether or not the agent is to be responsible for seeing that the goods or services comply with local regulations. This is important, because a UK business may not know about such requirements, and the purpose of appointing an agent is to increase business in other areas,

(7) whether or not the agent is to be allowed to

appoint sub-agents or to assign the agreement,

(8) details of marketing materials (brochures, samples, etc.) to be provided by the principal,

(9) advertising and marketing policy in the agent's territory,

(10) details of commission payable, how it is to be paid (e.g. invoice needed from the agent) and when (e.g. after the customer has paid),

(11) duration of the agreement and any rights of termination,

(12) if sales targets are not met, the principal may wish to be given the right to reduce the territory or range of goods and services in the agreement,

(13) whether or not the agent is allowed to represent competitors or sell competing products. Where an agent is regarded as an arm of the principal, many of the rules (see 3.3 below) affecting distributors to ensure that there are no restrictions on competition within the Community do not affect agencies. Otherwise, the European Court in *Suiker Unie v Commission* [1975] ECR 1663 has decided that such a restriction was acceptable provided that the agent was effectively an auxiliary to the principal's business. The relationship was akin to employer and employee. If, however, the agent sells the same product on his or her account to non-Member States, the restriction falls within Article 85 of the Treaty (see Appendix 2).

The subsequent written contract will contain a clause where the agent is expected not to give away any confidential information about his or her principal's affairs. If such details are likely to arise while the agreement is being negotiated, the agent must sign a confidentiality agreement before the talks begin. As the terms are often contained in a letter, the agent merely signs a copy of it and returns it to the prospective principal.

3.2.3 Other terms of an agency agreement

In addition to the points mentioned in the previous paragraph, the final agreement will contain other clauses not discussed during the negotiations, for instance:

(1) The agent will be expected to use 'best endeavours' to obtain sales. According to the law cases (such as *B. Davis v Tooth & Co* [1937] 4 All ER 118) this appears to mean that the agent will do what he or she reasonably could in the circumstances.

(2) The agent will not be allowed to make any terms other than those contained in his or her principal's contract of supply. Definitions of prohibited activities could include the granting of unauthorised discounts.

(3) It will be important to the principal that the agent describes himself or herself as an 'agent', and also makes clear the limitation of his or her authority to act on behalf of the principal.

(4) Confidential information about the principal will have to remain as such.

(5) The contract will have to contain a clause stating which law is to govern its interpretation. Principals based in England will normally want to have agreements governed by English law for the simple reason that they feel as though they know the rules. Some agents overseas may be able to force the principal to accept their own standard terms of agreement. If anything should go wrong the principal may be forced into finding a remedy through an unfamiliar system of law. The potential problems are noted in subsection *3.2.6* below.

(6) The contract will often state that it contains the entire agreement of the parties, and that any previous negotiations are invalid.

(7) If there are two versions of the contract in different languages, the governing version will have to be stated.

(8) Things can of course go wrong, so the agreement

will provide for various eventualities. It will, for example, usually be ended if either party should become insolvent. Most contracts will provide for disputes to be settled by one of the cheaper and easier arbitration procedures that are available. Note, however, that the effects of Articles 2 and 5 of the European Judgments Convention of 1968 (incorporated into UK law by the Civil Jurisdiction and Judgments Act 1982) are to allow a defendant agent or principal to be sued in a State other than that of his or her permanent residence.

3.2.4 Agents holding goods on consignment

In order to increase sales through the employment of an agent, a principal may have to give some of the products to be sold to the agent. He or she will then have a buffer stock with which to fulfil orders. The standard agency agreement mentioned in the previous paragraph will then have to be tailored to meet this situation:

(1) Ways of ascertaining stock levels to be held by the agent will have to be listed.

(2) The agreement will have to state who is to pay for freight, storage and insurance.

(3) There will have to be detailed accounting provisions. For example, the agent will normally invoice the customer as sales agent, and then at specified times will be invoiced for the goods by the manufacturer.

(4) It is an essential part of such arrangements that the title to the goods remains with the principal.

3.2.5 Where to find agents

A business seeking to expand its business by appointing agents in other countries of the Common Market has first to find its agent. It will be looking for people or businesses with expertise in the product, selling and the relevant market.

The search will start in trade magazines, the Department of Trade, Chambers of Commerce, and British

Embassies in the countries concerned. Useful addresses will be found in Appendix 3.

Once prospective agents have been found, the principal will have to visit them. Points to be considered are:

(1) Has the agent relevant experience?

(2) Does the agent have sufficient resources with particular regard to selling, marketing and the handling of customer problems?

(3) If the principal does not speak the language of the agent's territory, does the agent speak English?

(4) Are the references (which must be obtained) satisfactory?

Smaller businesses may wish to rely totally on the local knowledge of the agent in relation to their marketing. He or she may assist in such areas as the translation of selling brochures and the placing of advertisements.

In many agency agreements the principal wishes to control these activities. In such instances the translation can be done in the UK, and the larger agencies will be able to help with advertising throughout the Common Market.

In any event, it is essential for these matters to be dealt with. Even if advertising is not needed, sales brochures should be translated into the language of the prospective customers. An agent will not be pleased to receive colourful brochures written in English which contain a badly typed translation on a plain sheet of paper. Packaging and instruction books in particular must be carefully translated into local languages.

It is also essential to build up a good personal relationship with the agent, and to react positively to his or her advice on modifications to the product or marketing activities.

3.2.6 Some potential pitfalls and how to avoid them

Although principals will usually insist that their own country's laws will govern the agreements with their agents, some of the latter may insist on their own contracts. The Council Directive on self-employed commercial agents is not yet in force, although the UK has to comply with it by 1 January 1994. The laws of the various Community States will therefore differ at least for a while after 1992.

For example, in Germany and France an agent is entitled to adjustment fees on the termination of the agreement. These are intended to compensate him or her for the business brought to the principal.

Some countries have different types of agency. In Germany, for example, the *Handelsvertreter* is an independent business person who represents several enterprises. He or she is a sub-class of agent known as a *Vermittlungsvertreter*.

France has *l'agent commercial*, who works independently on a commission basis. There is also the VRP (*Voyageur, Représentant, Placier*) who is actually paid a salary or commission or both. He or she, however, is entitled to such benefits as a statutory notice period and compensation for loss of goodwill (similar to the German adjustment fees just mentioned).

Legal advice must therefore be taken before an agent is appointed.

3.2.7 Opportunities for agents

The Single Market in Europe also opens up opportunities for agents in the UK, because businesses in other countries will be influenced by all the propaganda of their own governments and will be looking for export possibilities. They too will be looking for agents in the UK to sell their products here.

In order to take advantage of this the agent will have to ensure that prospective principals are either contacted or have a chance of making contact. Larger agency firms can afford to undertake market research, either by employing researchers or by sending their own people abroad. Their marketing activities can concentrate on likely principals, and their representatives may be able to call on them.

Smaller agencies may have to rely on less direct methods. Advertising in trade magazines, contact with British Embassies overseas and membership of the relevant Chambers of Commerce can all help. Some useful addresses are contained in Appendix 3.

Once contact has been made, the agent should visit the prospective principal in order to discover whether or not he or she has sufficient resources to back up the sales effort. If the goods are of a technical nature, the principal will be able to provide sufficient back-up. Visits to existing customers should be made wherever possible.

References will be essential, and the agent must check the principal's credit rating in the usual way. This includes a banker's reference, which can be obtained through the agent's bank in the UK. In the request for such a reference the amount of any credit, i.e. the estimated commission likely to be owed, must be mentioned. The two requests for trade references should also be specific, and should ask for the following details:

(1) the length of time the referee has done business with the principal,

(2) the length of credit normally granted to the principal,

(3) the amount currently owed by the principal to the referee,

(4) the last time a transaction went through the account,

(5) the date of the oldest invoice currently unpaid.

It is good practice to obtain new trade and bank references every year or so, because circumstances can change.

Another useful guide to the capabilities of an agent is its accounts, which should be obtained wherever possible. Where it is a company, it is possible to search official records, and there are many international companies which can obain such information. It is best to give the accounts to an accountant capable of analysing and reporting on them. Large firms of accountants can give such a service, but smaller practices may not be so skilled.

If all goes well, a contract will have to be agreed. The points mentioned in *3.2.2* and *3.2.3* above should be noted.

3.3 Distributorships

3.3.1 Definition of a distributor

Some businesspeople refer to their distributors as 'agents', often because of the close relationship they have. A distributor, however, actually buys the goods and sells them as a wholesaler or retailer to its own customers. Its supplier will in many cases wish to restrict the distributor's freedom to sell competitive products. Another important restriction found in distributorship agreements is that of preventing the sale by the distributor of the goods to territories other than the one specified.

3.3.2 Regulations governing exclusive distributorships

Any restriction on the distributor in relation to its freedom to act in business is technically a breach of Article 85 of the Treaty. This is mentioned in more detail in Appendix 2. On the other hand, a distributor can help many suppliers and manufacturers to increase the market for their goods. Both aspects have been recognised by the Commission in Regulation 1983/83 concerning the application of Article 85(3) to exclusive distribution agreements. The main points are as follows:

(1) The exemption to the rules only apply if the agreement is between two undertakings only 'whereby one party agrees with the other to supply certain goods for resale within the whole or a defined area of the common market only to that other' (Article 1).

(2) The permitted restrictions are (a) not to manufacture or distribute competitive products, (b) only

to buy the goods for resale from the other party, and (c) not to seek customers for the goods outside the territory nor to establish branches or distribution branches for such goods outside that area. This obviously does not prevent the distributor from doing other businesss.

(3) Manufacturers of identical goods are not allowed to set up reciprocal distribution agreements with each other (Article 3(a)).

(4) Non-reciprocal distribution agreements in respect of such goods between such manufacturers are only exempt from the provisions of Article 85 of the Treaty if one of them has an annual turnover of no more than 100 million ECU (European Currency Units) (Article 3(b)).

(5) Distributorship agreements where the supplier is the sole source of the goods in the contract territory and the distributor has no alternatives outside are also not exempt from Article 85 of the Treaty (Article 3(c)).

(6) Other distribution agreements are also not exempt, where either of the parties makes it difficult to obtain alternative sources of supply, either in the Common Market or outside it, if there is no such internal source. The use by a supplier of an industrial property right such as a trade mark is also prohibited, and is intended to cover a situation like that in *Etablissements Consten SA and Grundig-Verkaufs GmbH v EEC* [1966] 1 CMLR 428. The supplier allotted different trade marks for each territory, so that if a distributor sold into the territory of another, it would infringe the trade mark of the latter.

(7) Article 6 permits the EEC Commission to withdraw the block exemption in certain situations, which in principle are incompatible with Article 85(3) of the Treaty. This relates to goods where there are no effective alternative sources of supply, or

where the distributor sells at excessively high prices, or unjustifiably limits the sale of the goods to persons without such alternative sources.

(8) The Regulation does not apply to the resale of drinks in premises used for the sale and consumption of beer or to the resale of petroleum products in service stations (Article 8).

(9) The Regulation will expire at the end of 1997, and itself is a replacement of the earlier Regulation No. 67/67, which also gave a block exemption to such agreements under similar terms.

3.3.3 Non-exclusive distributorships

Provided that all other aspects relating to the ban on anti-competitive practices are complied with, non-exclusive distributorships are obviously not prohibited.

3.3.4 Terms of a distributorship – a check list

Although a distributorship agreement should be drafted by a lawyer, for the purposes of negotiating the deal the prospective principal (or agent) should have a check list of the points to be covered. They should include:

(1) the correct names and addresses of the parties – trading names are not enough,

(2) whether or not the agreement is to be exclusive as to territory. This should be clearly stated,

(3) the territory in which the goods or services are to be sold. Very often there are provisions to review the extent of the territory should sales targets not be achieved,

(4) a description of the goods. Very often there is a provision to reduce the range to be offered to the distributor should sales targets not be met,

(5) details of any training to be provided for the distributor,

(6) whether or not the distributor is to be allowed to appoint agents or to assign the agreement,

(7) details of marketing materials (brochures, samples, etc.) to be provided by the principal.

Because the distributor will effectively be doing his or her own marketing, the supplier usually insists on giving approval to any advertising campaign or will participate in it,

(8) price of the goods, which is sometimes expressed as a percentage of the supplier's list price. The distributor may be entitled to volume discounts,

(9) duration of the agreement and any rights of termination.

Distributorship agreements also cover other points:

(1) the principal will usually agree to submit any orders from persons within the distributor's territory to the distributor, although this will not apply to non-exclusive agreements,

(2) the distributor is usually made responsible for seeing that the goods comply with local regulations. On the other hand the supplier will be expected to cooperate and ensure that any necessary changes are made,

(3) the distributor will normally be expected to provide forecasts of expected demand,

(4) the distributor may be expected to provide an after-sales service.

3.3.5 Other terms of a distributorship agreement

The subsequent written contract will contain a clause where the distributor is expected not to give away any confidential information about his or her supplier's affairs. If such details are likely to arise while the agreement is being negotiated, the distributor must sign a confidentiality agreement before they start. As this often takes the form of a letter, the distributor merely signs a copy of it and returns it to the prospective supplier.

In addition to these points, the final agreement will contain other clauses not discussed during the negotiations, such as:

(1) The distributor will be expected to use 'best endeavours' to promote and extend sales of the

products in the territory. According to the law cases (such as *B. Davis v Tooth & Co* [1937] 4 All ER 118) this appears to mean that the distributor will do what he or she reasonably could in the circumstances.

(2) The distributor will not be allowed to sell the goods on terms more favourable to a sub-purchaser or more detrimental to the supplier than those contained in that supplier's contract of supply.

(3) The supplier may still want an exclusive distributor to describe his or her self as a 'selling agent'. This may arise out of a mistaken view of the relationship, and also out of the exclusivity of the agreement. The distributor, for example, may not stock any other products. Distributors should be wary of adopting these words, because there may be legal implications. The agreement itself will usually state quite clearly state that an agency is not being created.

(4) Confidential information about the supplier will have to remain as such.

(5) The contract will have to contain a clause stating which law is to govern its interpretation. Suppliers based in England will normally want to have agreements governed by English law for the simple reason that they feel as though they know the rules. Some distributors overseas may be able to force the supplier to accept their own standard terms of agreement. If anything should go wrong, the supplier may be forced into finding a remedy through an unfamiliar system of law. The potential problems are noted in subsection *3.3.7* below.

(6) The contract will often state that it contains the entire agreement of the parties, and that any previous negotiations are invalid.

(7) If there are two versions of the contract in different languages, the governing version will have to be stated.

(8) Things can of course go wrong, so the agreement will provide for various eventualities. It will, for example, usually be ended if either party should become insolvent. Most contracts will provide for disputes to be settled by one of the cheaper and easier arbitration procedures that are available.

3.3.6 Where to find distributors

A business seeking to expand its business by appointing distributors in other countries of the Common Market has first to find its distributor. It will be looking for people or businesses with expertise in the product, selling and the relevant market.

The search will start in trade magazines, the Department of Trade, Chambers of Commerce, and British Embassies in the countries concerned. Useful addresses will be found in Appendix 3.

Once prospective distributors have been found, the supplier will have to visit them. Points to be considered are:

(1) Has the distributor relevant experience?

(2) Does the distributor have sufficient resources with particular regard to selling, marketing and the handling of customer problems?

(3) Does the distributor have sufficient resources to comply with health and safety rules?

(4) If the supplier does not speak the language of the distributor's territory, does the supplier speak English?

(5) Are the references (which must be obtained) satisfactory?

References will be essential, and the supplier must check the distributor's credit rating in the usual way. This includes a banker's reference, which can be obtained through the principal's bank in the UK. In the request for such a reference the amount of any credit limit must be mentioned. The two requests for trade references should also be specific, and ask for the following details:

(1) the length of time the referee has done business with the distributor,

(2) the length of credit normally granted to the distributor,

(3) the amount currently owed by the distributor to the referee,

(4) the last time a transaction went through the account,

(5) the date of the oldest invoice currently unpaid.

It is good practice to obtain new bank and trade references every year or so, because circumstances can change.

Another useful guide to the capabilities of a distributor is its accounts, which should be obtained wherever possible. Where it is a company, it is possible to search official records, and there are many international companies which can obain such information. It is best to give the accounts to an accountant capable of analysing and reporting on them. Large firms of accountants can give such a service, but smaller practices may not be so skilled.

The supplier, particularly if it is a small or medium-sized company, may have to rely on the distributor's expertise and knowledge of the territory. Packaging may well have to be changed, and some electrical equipment, for example, may have to be supplied with an electric plug already fitted. Brochures and instruction booklets will have to be translated into the relevant languages.

3.3.7 Some potential pitfalls and how to avoid them

Some of the potential pitfalls have been mentioned in the previous chapter in the section relating to Articles 85 and 86 of the Treaty. National laws of Member States can throw up some surprises.

Distributors in Belgium, for example, have statutory protection in relation to the termination of their contracts under Loi du 27 Juillet 1961 as amended by Loi du 13 Avril 1971. Reasonable notice must be given if the supplier wishes to terminate the agreement other than for the failure of the distributor to comply with its terms, or mutual agreement to end it, or in accordance with one of its provisions. The law states that if the distributorship relates to all or part of Belgium, and the distributor brings any action in relation to the termination before a Belgian court, that court will apply Belgian law. In other words, these provisions cannot be avoided.

Distributorship agreements in relation to other countries should therefore be drafted by legal experts.

3.3.8 Opportunities for distributors

The points relating to agents in subsection *3.2.7* above apply equally to distributors in the UK.

3.4	# Model agency and distributorship agreements

3.4.1 General points

One objection made by businesspeople to contracts prepared by lawyers is that they look very formal. Marketing people may have spent plenty of time cultivating a potential distributor or agent with the aid of glossy brochures and sales talk, but the deal is then formalised with a document that frightens the other party to go and see his or her own lawyer with consequent delay.

There must, however, be an agreement, which will be needed if the relationship turns sour. A compromise is to present the agreement in the form of a letter of appointment for the agent or distributor to sign and return. Although the main terms should be drafted by a lawyer, the marketing people can at least write the first and last paragraphs in a less formal style.

The following paragraphs consequently contain examples of agency and distributor agreements. They must never be copied slavishly, but must be tailored to fit the commercial situation. That is why a lawyer should be

instructed to draft the main terms. Use of the check lists in
3.2.2 and *3.3.4* will, however, save time and money.

3.4.2 A model letter appointing an exclusive agent

Dear

Now that you have seen our range of products and
talked with us, I think you will agree that they offer many
opportunities for you. The purpose of this letter is therefore
to appoint your company ABC Limited ('the Agent') as the
agent of XYZ Limited ('the Company') subject to your
formal acceptance, and to set out the terms as follows:

1   The territory ('the Territory') covered by this Agreement
shall be

2   The products ('the Products') covered by this Agreement
shall be those in the trade catalogue of the Company ruling
at any particular time.

3   This Agreement shall commence on
and shall expire two years after commencement subject to
prior termination as provided hereunder.

4   The Company shall not appoint any other persons to act
as its agent in the Territory for the products during the
currency of this Agreement, except that during any period
of notice of termination given by either party in accordance
with the terms herein the Company may appoint the
Agent's successor and allow such agent to make itself
known as the Company's agent able to do business from a
specific date being not earlier than the day after the
expiration or termination hereof.

5   The Agent shall:
>   (a) use its best endeavours to promote and extend the
>   sale of the Products throughout the Territory, will
>   study and keep under review market conditions and
>   the competition to ascertain the most likely areas
>   where or classes of persons to whom sales may be
>   made and will endeavour to obtain orders;

(b) give proper consideration and weight to the Company in all dealings and abide by any rules or instructions notified by the Company to the Agent;

(c) not sell or assist any other persons to sell (whether directly or indirectly) goods of the same description as the Products or which perform the same function;

(d) not without the prior written consent of the Company knowingly sell or supply to any person Products which are intended for export outside the Territory;

(e) promptly refer to the Company all enquiries for any of the Products for supply outside the Territory without being entitled to commission thereon;

(f) not make any representations or give any warranties or other benefits in favour of any proposed purchaser or to the detriment of the Company beyond those contained in the Company's standard conditions of sale ruling at the time;

(g) in the event of any dispute arising between the Agent and any proposed purchaser in relation to the sale or offer for sale of any of the Products forthwith inform the Company of the details and the circumstances of the dispute and shall not without the prior written consent of the Company institute proceedings in respect of the dispute or compromise the same or release any debtor;

(h) promptly inform the Company of any facts or opinions likely to be relevant in relation to the marketing of any of the Products and any use or resale thereof which is advantageous or disadvantageous to the Company;

(i) ensure that the Company is informed of all local regulations in relation to health and safety or any other matter relating to any of the Products and shall not take orders for any of the Products which would contravene such regulations;

(j) keep detailed records of all the transactions

relating to the Agent's activities on behalf of the Company;

(k) maintain a separate bank account in respect of money received from sales of any of the Products on behalf of the Company and will remit to the Company by not later than the first day of the month following the receipt of such money all sums received less any commission agreed by the Company to be due to the Agent;

(m) supply the Company with reports returns and other information requested by the Company;

(n) not appoint sub-agents or assign transfer charge (or purport to do the same) all or any part of this Agreement or any rights thereunder;

(o) not alter remove or tamper with the marks, trade marks, numbers or other means of identification on any of the Company's Products;

(p) not act in any manner which will expose the Company to any liability nor pledge or purport to pledge the Company's credit;

(q) in all correspondence, commercial documents and on any relevant posters, brochures or any other advertising material in relation to any of the Products describe itself as 'selling agent' or 'selling agents' for the Company and will take all necessary steps to make clear the extent of the limitation of its authority to act on behalf of the Company;

(r) defray all expenses of and incidental to the agency hereunder incurred by the Agent;

(s) maintain sufficient trained staff in relation both to selling any of the Products and to answering enquiries from customers or users in the Territory;

(t) send such sales staff as the Company shall direct on training courses run by the Company at the Company's expense;

(u) not divulge any information in relation to the Company which is confidential to any third party and this obligation shall survive the termination or expiration of this Agreement.

6   The Company shall be responsible for advertising in the Territory and shall supply leaflets, instruction books and brochures in the language of the Territory.

7   It is hereby acknowledged that any trade marks used on or in association with the Products are the property of the Company and the Agent will take all steps as are practicable to ensure that the property in the trade marks in the Territory shall vest in and remain vested in the Company. Where the Company wishes to make an application for the registration of the trade mark in the Territory the Agent shall give reasonable assistance to the Company in connection therewith. Should it be necessary to register the trade mark in the name of the Agent then the Agent shall make such registration at the expense of the Company and promptly assign it to the Company.

8   The Agent shall be entitled to a commission of x% on the value excluding VAT and transportation charges of any invoice to a customer from whom the Agent has obtained an order in the Territory. Such commission shall be paid by not later than the month following the month in which the customer has paid against any such invoice.

9   Either party may terminate this Agreement:
    (a) at any time after the expiration of one year from the date of commencement of this Agreement by giving to the other not less than three months' notice in writing; or
    (b) forthwith if the other party commits a breach of any of the terms of this Agreement and fails to remedy the same (where it is capable of being remedied) within the period specified within a notice given by the aggrieved party to the party in default calling for a remedy, being a period not less than thirty days; or

(c) forthwith if the other party becomes insolvent or has a receiver appointed of any of its assets or execution or distress is levied on such assets; or

(d) forthwith if an order is made or a resolution is passed for a winding-up or liquidation of the other party (except where any such event is only for the purposes of amalgamation with another or recon-struction and the resultant company agrees to be bound by the terms hereof); or

(e) forthwith if the other party should cease trading.

10 If the Agreement should be terminated the Agent shall only be entitled to the minimum compensation stipulated by law.

11 For a period of two years after the expiration or termination of this Agreement the Agent shall not be associated whether as principal or agent in the manufac-ture, sale or distribution in the Territory of goods of the same or similar description of any of the Products or those which perform a similar function.

12 The Company shall not be liable to the Agent for any failure to supply any of the Products to a customer in accordance with an order obtained by the Agent.

13 The Company may set sales targets to be achieved by the Agent, and may reduce the area of the Territory or the range of the Products or both should the Agent fail to meet those targets.

14 This Agreement shall be governed and interpreted in accordance with English law. Any dispute which cannot be resolved by the parties shall be referred to arbitration in London in accordance with the provisions of the Ar-bitration Acts 1950–1975.

15 If any term of this Agreement is in conflict with national law or public policy the validity of the whole will not be affected by the omission of the conflicting re-quirement.

Please therefore sign the copy of this letter to signify your acceptance of its terms, and return it to us.

Yours . . . . ,

For and on behalf of . . . .

Name of signatory

Job title of signatory

We hereby agree to the terms contained in this letter.

Signed . . . . .Date . . . .

for and on behalf of . . . .(name of company)

Job title of signatory . . . .

Name of signatory (block capitals) . . . .

3.4.3 A model letter appointing an exclusive distributor

Dear

Now that you have seen our range of products and talked with us, I think you will agree that they offer many opportunities for you. The purpose of this letter is therefore to appoint your company ABC Limited ('the Distributor') as the agent of XYZ Limited ('the Company') subject to your formal acceptance, and to set out the terms as follows:

1 The territory ('the Territory') covered by this Agreement shall be

2 The products ('the Products') covered by this Agreement shall be those in the trade catalogue of the Company ruling at any particular time.

3 This Agreement shall commence on
and shall expire two years after commencement subject to prior termination as provided hereunder.

4   The Company shall not appoint any other persons to act as its distributor in the Territory for the products during the currency of this Agreement, except that during any period of notice of termination given by either party in accordance with the terms herein the Company may appoint the Distributor's successor and allow such distributor to make itself known as the Company's distributor able to do business from a specific date being not earlier than the day after the expiration or termination hereof.

5   If by reason of a European Economic Community directive regulation legislation or the like or of a relevant national law as a result of such such directive regulation legislation or the like, the Company should be unable to refuse a request from a third party for a distributorship of any of the Products in the Territory the Company shall notify the Distributor without delay.

6   The Company may set sales targets to be achieved by the Distributor, and may reduce the area of the Territory or the range of the Products or both should the Distributor fail to meet those targets.

7   The Company shall not be either under an obligation to manufacture the Products or prevented from making alterations to the design production packaging or design of any of the Products.

8   The Company shall not be liable to the Distributor should any third party import any of the Products into the Territory and offer the same for sale therein.

9   The Company shall use its best endeavours to supply any of the Products in accordance with the Distributor's orders in so far as it is not prevented by reasons beyond its control including limitations of availability, production hold-ups, labour disputes, bad weather conditions and the like. In the event of such happenings the Company shall fulfil the Distributor's orders pro rata with orders from other customers.

10   All transactions for the sale of any of the Products by

the Company to the Distributor shall be in accordance with the Company's standard terms and conditions of sale at the time any order from the Distributor is accepted by the Company.

11 All orders received by the Company from customers in the Territory shall be referred to the Distributor.

12 The prices of the Products ordered by the Distributor shall be those ex works prices contained in the Company's trade catalogue at the time of supply less a discount of 20%. The Distributor shall pay for all freight delivery and insurance charges. The time of payment shall be in accordance with the Company's standard terms and conditions of sale at the time an order was placed by the Distributor.

13 The Company at its own expense shall supply training to such of the Distributor's staff as it deems to be necessary.

14 The Distributor shall:

(a) use its best endeavours to promote and extend the sale of the Products throughout the Territory, will study and keep under review market conditions and the competition to ascertain the most likely areas where or classes of persons to whom sales may be made and will endeavour to obtain orders;

(b) give proper consideration and weight to the Company in all dealings and abide by any rules or instructions notified by the Company to the Distributor;

(c) not sell or assist any other persons to sell (whether directly or indirectly) goods of the same description as the Products or those which perform the same function;

(d) not make any representations or give any warranties or other benefits in favour of any proposed purchaser or to the detriment of the Company beyond those contained in the Company's standard conditions of sale ruling at the time;

(e) in the event of any dispute arising between the

Distributor and any proposed purchaser in relation to the sale or offer for sale of any of the Products forthwith inform the Company of the details and the circumstances of the dispute and shall not without the prior written consent of the Company institute proceedings in respect of the dispute or compromise the same or release any debtor;

(f)   promptly inform the Company of any facts or opinions likely to be relevant in relation to the marketing of any of the Products and any use or resale thereof which is advantageous or disadvantageous to the Company;

(g)   ensure that the Company is informed of all local regulations in relation to health and safety or any other matter relating to any of the Products and shall not take orders for any of the Products which would contravene such regulations;

(h)   supply the Company with reports, returns and other information requested by the Company;

(i)   not alter, remove or tamper with the marks, trade marks, numbers or other means of identification on any of the Company's Products;

(j)   not act in any manner which will expose the Company to any liability;

(k)   in all correspondence, commercial documents and on any relevant posters, brochures or any other advertising material in relation to any of the Products describe itself as 'selling agent' or 'selling agents' for the Company and will take all necessary steps to make clear the extent of the limitation of its authority to act on behalf of the Company;

(l)   defray all expenses of and incidental to the distributorship hereunder incurred by the Distributor;

(m) maintain sufficient trained staff in relation to selling any of the Products responding to enquiries from customers or users in the Territory and provide an adequate after-sales service;

(n) maintain adequate stocks both of the Product to satisfy orders and of spare parts;

(p) not divulge any information in relation to the Company which is confidential to any third party and this obligation shall survive the termination or expiration of this Agreement;

(q) be responsible for marketing the Products within the Territory.

15 Neither party may assign all or any part of this Agreement.

16 Either party may terminate this Agreement:

(a) at any time after the expiration of one year from the date of commencement of this Agreement by giving to the other not less than three months' notice in writing; or

(b) forthwith if the other party commits a breach of any of the terms of this Agreement and fails to remedy the same (where it is capable of being remedied) within the period specified within a notice given by the aggrieved party to the party in default calling for a remedy, being a period not less than thirty days; or

(c) forthwith if the other party becomes insolvent, or has a receiver appointed of any of its assets, or execution or distress is levied on such assets; or

(d) forthwith if an order is made or a resolution is passed for a winding-up or liquidation of the other party (except where any such event is only for the purposes of amalgamation with another or reconstruction and the resultant company agrees to be bound by the terms hereof); or

(e) forthwith if the other party should cease trading.

17 The relationship between the parties is that of seller and buyer under an exclusive supply agreement.

18 This Agreement shall be governed and interpreted in accordance with English law. Any dispute which cannot be

resolved by the parties shall be referred to arbitration in London in accordance with the provisions of the Arbitration Acts 1950–1975.

19 If any term of this Agreement is in conflict with national law or public policy the validity of the whole will not be affected by the omission of the conflicting requirement.

Please therefore sign the copy of this letter to signify your acceptance of its terms, and return it to us.

Yours . . . . ,

For and on behalf of . . . .

Name of signatory

Job title of signatory

We hereby agree to the terms contained in this letter.

Signed . . . . .Date . . . .

for and on behalf of . . . .(name of company)

Job title of signatory . . . .

Name of signatory (block capitals) . . . .

3.5 Know-how licensing agreements

3.5.1 The general rules

Know-how licensing agreements may be a way to obtain a royalty for a good idea, but they can also be a restraint on trade. The licensor might impose too wide restrictions on the field of use of the know-how. Other restraints on the expiry of the agreement may be too wide. The Commission is issuing a regulation on the application of Article 85(3) to such contracts.

The regulation is complicated so it is only possible to list some of the main provisions:

(1) The agreement must be between two undertakings only.

(2) Details of the know-how must be recorded in a separate document or some other form (e.g. a computer record).

(3) The usual clauses in a know-how licence agreement are permitted, e.g. no sub-licensing, improvements in the process to be notified to the other party, the licensee to purchase such supplies from the licensor as are necessary for a technically satisfactory exploitation of the licensed technology.

(4) A licensee can be directed to pay royalties for up to three years after the know-how has come into public knowledge through the action of third parties.

(5) Some restrictions are not permitted such as one preventing the licensee from using the know-how after it has come into the public domain. The licensee furthermore may not be forced to assign to the licensor any rights in improvements to the know-how. Clauses restricting the prices charged for the ultimate product are not allowed.

(6) In keeping with the spirit of the Community the agreement may not restrict competition between the parties.

(7) Know-how licensing agreements between competitors who hold interests in a joint venture, or between one of them and that joint venture, are not allowed if the licensing activities relate to the joint venture.

(8) The Commission may withdraw the benefit of the Regulation if it is being used in such a way as to restrict competition. An example is where one or both of the parties unreasonably refuses to sell to prospective buyers in their respective territories, where those purchasers would resell into other parts of the Common Market.

3.5.2 A check list for licensors

A licensor who wishes to receive royalties from selling his or her know-how must obviously find out more about the licensee. There could be unpleasant consequences if he or she does nothing.

(1) Has a secrecy agreement or letter been signed? All negotiations about know-how and patents should be subject to such an agreement.

(2) Does the licensee have sufficient resources to use the know-how effectively?

(3) Will the know-how, the licensee or the resulting product comply with all relevant health and safety regulations?

(4) Does the licensee have sufficient resources to market the resulting product effectively?

(5) References must be obtained both from the licensee's bank and at least two of its trade creditors. The requests should follow the guidelines mentioned in *3.3.6* above.

(6) Does the licensee have an adequate after-sales service?

3.5.3 An agreement check list

A licensing agreement is best left to a specialist in this field, but much time and money can be saved if the essentials of the deal are agreed during the negotiations. A check list must include:

(1) the correct names and business addresses of the parties (plus registered offices if relevant),

(2) the nature of the know-how to be licensed,

(3) to whom the know-how may be disclosed and any restrictions arising out of confidentiality,

(4) training in the know-how's use and any special procedures to be followed,

(5) any terms relating to the use of trade marks and trade names,

(6) the procedure if either party should improve the subject matter of the know-how agreement. Most

contracts state that the improver will notify the other party, and a decision will be made by the licensor about whether or not to apply for a patent,

(7) the royalties payable,

(8) the duration of the agreement.

3.5.4 Know-how: an opportunity for licensees

Another means of expansion is to buy know-how. Businesses may discover such opportunities through their membership of trade associations and the like, but prospective licensors sometimes advertise through journals published by overseas' Chambers of Commerce. Some useful addresses will be found in Appendix 3.

3.5.5 A disclosure letter

Before negotiations begin a prospective licensor must obtain a promise from the hopeful licensee, that the latter will not disclose any confidential information that might consequently be revealed. Such a letter should be drafted by a lawyer, but a possible approach is as follows:

Dear

Because we are about to enter into negotiations about the possible licensing of know-how, it is obviously important that any information we reveal should be kept confidential. We are therefore prepared to proceed in accordance with the following terms and conditions:

(1) In consideration of your entering into negotiations ('the Negotiations') with us about the possible licensing of our know-how to you in the area of ('the Know-how') we shall reveal to you sufficient information ('the Information') as we shall deem necessary for you to evaluate it.

(2) You agree that you will not without our prior written consent make any notes, sketches, drawings, photographs or copies of any kind of the Information.

(3) You shall not disclose the Information to anyone other than those of your employees named below:

('the Employees')

(4) You shall keep the Information secret and shall not reveal the same to any third party unless and until it has become part of the public domain.

(5) You shall ensure that the Employees shall be bound by the terms of this letter.

(6) At the end of the Negotiations you shall promptly or at such time as we shall request, return any notes, sketches, drawings, photographs or copies of any kind of the Information in your possession.

Please therefore sign the copy of this letter in the space provided to signify your acceptance of these terms and conditions, and return it to us.

Yours . . . . ,

For and on behalf of . . . .

Name of signatory

Job title of signatory

We hereby agree to the terms and conditions contained in this letter.

Signed . . . . .Date . . . .

for and on behalf of . . . .(name of company)

Job title of signatory . . . .

Name of signatory (block capitals) . . . .

3.6 | Trade marks

Another means of obtaining royalties is from the licensing of a trade mark. This is usually done in the context of a know-how or patent licensing agreement, so the points made in the preceding paragraph apply. An important extra consideration is whether or not a trade mark is valid or registrable in the territory where it is being licensed. Advice must be sought from a Trade Mark Agent.

3.7 | Patents

There are many parallels between the licensing of patents and of know-how. Patents, however, enjoy much better legal protection for a specific time, provided that they have been registered in the territory where they are to be exploited. Any business with a new idea has to be quick off the mark, or it will not gain protection. Immediate advice must be obtained from a Patent Agent.

3.8 | Copyright

Another means of obtaining royalty income is by selling rights in a design. In the UK it is possible to register a non-functional design for a limited period (fifteen years in respect of an industrially applied design (s 1 Registered Designs Act 1949).

3.9 | Franchising

3.9.1 The rules

A popular means of expanding a business idea is by means of franchising, but the nature of the operation, such as exclusive buying, could be regarded as a restraint on competition. The Commission has therefore issued a Regulation governing the situation.

Article 1 defines a franchising agreement as one 'whereby one undertaking, the franchisor, grants the other, the franchisee, in exchange for direct or indirect financial consideration, the right to exploit a franchise for the purposes of marketing specified types of goods and/or services'. It adds that 'a franchise means a package of industrial or intellectual property rights relating to trade marks, trade names, shop signs, utility models, designs, copyrights, know-how or patents, to be exploited for the resale of goods or the provision of services to end users ...'

The Regulation permits the usual clauses that appear in franchise agreements such as the maintenance of the franchisor's quality standards and secrecy in relation to any know-how.

The franchisee must, however, among other things:

(1) be free to purchase the goods from other franchisees,

(2) be free to acquire a financial interest in (but not control over) competitors,

(3) ensure that the know-how and other rights are detailed in a document agreed by both the parties.

As might be expected reciprocal franchising agreements in respect of identical goods are not allowed. The franchisee must be free to decide its own resale prices.

3.9.2 Practical aspects

A prospective franchisee must research the franchise properly. He or she should therefore inspect other franchise outlets and obtain trade and bank references. Copies of the latest accounts should be obtained and given to an accountant capable of doing an analysis. Larger firms can provide such a service, but smaller firms may not have the requisite skills. Market research and a business plan (see in particular chapters 2 and 10) are essential.

A new franchisor should at least have its own pilot operation open for business and inspection. It too should check that prospective franchisees have personal resources and business skills to operate the outlet.

3.10 | Opportunities for business

In summary:

(1) Two means of increasing business and taking advantage of the atmosphere of a Single European Market are the appointments either of agents or of distributors, subject to the competition rules.

(2) For technically innovative businesses for whom marketing in other countries is not practicable, licensing of know-how, patents, trade marks and copyright is an opportunity to increase their profits

from royalties. The EEC Regulation mentioned in 3.5 above provides useful guidelines as to what is permissible in respect of know-how.

(3) A company with a bright marketing idea could also expand by means of franchising, but would also be well advised to follow the recommendations of the British Franchising Association as well as adopt the form of agreement contained in the Commission's Regulation noted in 3.9 above.

The key to success is obtaining the right information, but each sector of the business economy is different. Specific information will have to be researched, and the addresses in Appendix 3 will provide a starting point towards expansion. Businesses which ignore the Common Market may find they cannot withstand new competition from more enterprising companies in the Community.

CHAPTER 4
Increased business through joint ventures, consultancies, acquisitions, mergers and takeovers

4.1 | Introduction

Opportunities for expansion can arise either through collaboration with overseas businesses or by a greater involvement abroad. The key to success in these areas is to work from the outset with a strong professional team of advisers, because of the complexities that can arise in setting up the right deal.

4.2	**Joint ventures**

4.2.1 Background

If two businesses get together with a view to setting up a joint venture, there is the danger that competition will be restricted. Some of the cases before the European Court are outlined in Appendix 2. On the other hand some research is so expensive, particularly for small companies, that shared effort may be beneficial.

This was recognised by the Commission in an announcement on 24 July 1968. It collectively thought that various agreements by small and medium-sized companies did not restrict competition. These include the following in the context of an agreement which has the sole object of:

(1) an exchange of opinion or know-how,

(2) joint market research,

(3) joint provision of credit guarantees,

(4) joint debt-collecting associations,

(5) joint implementation of research and development contracts,

(6) joint placing of such contracts,

(7) the sharing of such research and development projects among participating enterprises,

(8) joint use of production facilities,

(9) the setting up of working partnerships where the participants are not competitors,

(10) joint selling arrangements (subject to the points on competition mentioned in the previous chapter and under distributorships above),

(11) joint after-sales and repair service by non-competitors,

(12) common competitor labels.

The products in question must not exceed 15% of the market for such goods and the aggregate turnover of the participants must not exceed 300 million units of account.

4.2.2 Points to consider

Joint ventures in relation to the Common Market will probably only work, if the partners know each other. It is more likely that such collaboration will be carried out by businesses of the same nationality because of a common language.

A small or medium-sized company which has a bright idea beyond its existing resources, yet which could achieve the objective in collaboration with others, is also not likely to broadcast it generally. The bigger multi-nationals would take it over for themselves. The innovator is therefore not going to advertise that it is looking for a partner, so will quietly approach other businesses which are known to it.

There are, however, alternatives to this approach in the area of research and development. The European Community funds various research projects such as Framework in information technology and EUREKA in hi-tech goods and services. This latter programme also has the objective of bringing together projects and partners. The company with an innovative idea may, with the aid of funding, be able to collaborate with, say, a university to develop it. The EUREKA scheme could also bring together several small companies in a joint venture. The address of the EUREKA office is contained in Appendix 3.

4.2.3 Procedure

The first stage in the procedure is for the business with the bright idea to take some steps to test its viability as far as possible. This should involve some preliminary market research, perhaps with the aid of a grant as mentioned in section 4.3 below, and then the drafting of a business plan. This will be a mixture of:

(1) a selling document to interest people in the idea,
(2) a description of how the idea could be brought into being,
(3) a list of all the resources that will be needed,
(4) a financial plan.

The innovator will then have to investigate whether a joint venture or a scheme such as EUREKA (see subsection *4.2.2* above) is the right approach. Once the partners have been chosen, it is a job for a professional team, which will include the following:

(1) the experts and researchers who will guide the technical aspects of the project,

(2) the lawyers who will assist in the negotiation of the agreement, and will have the job of drafting some very complicated legal documents,

(3) the market researchers, who will test the viability of the idea,

(4) the accountants who will budget for the scheme and control expenditure,

(5) the directors or owners of the participants who will be taking the risk and ultimately be responsible for coordinating the project,

(6) someone who will have to be made responsible for coordinating these activities and assist in building up the team.

The plan can then be formalised and work can begin.

4.3 Consultancies

The Single European Market will give consultancies many opportunities:

(1) It will be easier than has been the case to set up offices in other Member States.

(2) For those people with scientific skills and qualifications such schemes as EUREKA mentioned in the previous paragraph mean that money is available for research. The Department of Trade and Industry can obviously help with information, and useful names and addresses will be found in Appendix 3.

(3) The Community has set up various Structural Funds, which will increase from £5 billion in 1987 to £9 billion in 1992 and to £18 billion in 1993. The main beneficiaries will be Portugal, Greece, Spain,

Italy and Ireland. The funds will give opportunities for consultants with various skills. Money, for example, has been made available through the ERDF scheme for businesses in certain regions of the UK, which require the assistance of consultants.

The funds are:
(1) ERDF (European Regional Development Fund) which is intended to help less-developed and declining industrial regions.
(2) ESF (European Social Fund) which is particularly concerned with vocational guidance and training, retraining and job creation.
(3) FEOGA (European Agricultural Guidance and Guarantee Fund) which is intended to assist farmers in less favoured areas.
(4) IMPS (Integrated Mediterranean Programmes) – intended to help the countries bordering the Mediterranean.
(5) PEDIP (Programme for Modernisation of Portuguese Industry) which is intended to help modernise Portuguese industry.

Consultants with relevant qualifications may be able to help even where the fund is intended to help a specific region. They will also benefit from the elimination of national barriers relating to public purchasing, although of course the consultants with the relevant languages as well as skills will be more favoured with the business. Addresses of the various funds are mentioned in Appendix 3, while in the UK consultants may take advantage of the DTI Enterprise Initiative Scheme. Businesses under this scheme receive grants towards the cost of consultancy fees.

4.4 Acquisitions, mergers and takeovers

Any acquisition, merger or takeover is a complicated matter and requires the help of lawyers and accountants. A broker and a merchant bank has to be added to this mixture if the transaction has to be put to shareholders at an extraordinary general meeting, such as in a takeover of a company whose shares are quoted on a Stock Exchange. Instead of a merchant bank some larger accountancy firms can give support to prospective purchasers of a target company. Indeed, in the context of Europe they may have a stronger presence throughout the Community than merchant banks.

If part of the strategy for expansion involves the strengthening of the home market through the acquisition of a UK company, the situation is complicated. The rules are at least laid down in the Stock Exchange Yellow and Blue Books, while queries can be referred to the Take Over Panel.

There is, however, no pan-European equivalent of those rules, and according to Robert Swannell of Schroders (as reported in *Acquisitions Monthly* February 1989), 'We are going to have some significant easing of these obstacles before we can expect anything like the sort of M&A (merger and acquisition) activity found in the UK or US'. Although UK bidders made 253 bids worth £2,610 million into other Community countries in 1988, businesses from those countries made 103 bids worth the much higher £5,153 million into the UK.

This is not to say there is no regulation at all. In France the *Commission des Opérations de Bourse* controls the information given to shareholders as well as the function of the stock exchanges. Small shareholders, for example, representing at least 10% of their company's capital may petition a court of law to appoint an expert. That expert will report on the company's operations in accordance with the guidelines laid down by the court.

In the sense of a realization that there should be some sort of regulation, there is some movement towards harmonisation. UK law had to be changed in order to divide companies into those with plc (public limited company) after their names and those which were merely limited. In

Germany the equivalents are *Aktiengesellschaft* (AG) and the *Gesellschaft mit beschränkter Haftung* (GmbH).

This emphasises the need both for expert professionals and for patience when implementing a policy of acquiring, merging with, or taking over a quoted company in another country. The high-street firm of solicitors, for example, is unlikely to have sufficient expertise in this area either in the UK or other countries. The law society can help with names and addresses of those which do. Similar considerations apply to accountants, and only larger firms will have the right experience.

Another complicating factor is that mergers could be caught by the restrictions relating to an abuse of a dominant postion (Article 86 of the EEC Treaty). According to Lord Jauncey in the Court of Session case *Argyll Group plc v The Distillers Company plc* [1986] 1 CMLR 764 this meant 'a significant and abnormal effect upon the market to the extent that the degree of competition is not only altered thereby but is distorted in a manner which could only be achieved by the exercise of a dominant position'. All this seems to mean is that the judges are as confused as everyone else.

It is obviously easier to buy into a private company, a partnership or a sole trader's business. One option, of course, is to buy what is left of the business of a company in liquidation or receivership. Care must obviously be taken to ensure that the business can be made profitable.

All this means that it is difficult for UK companies to acquire, merge with, or take over a business in another Member State, although some companies in the UK could themselves be the target of a takeover bid. The directors of companies with large numbers of shareholders should consult with their brokers about possible defence strategies.

4.5 | **Opportunities for business**

The consequences of the Single Market in Europe on the topics covered in this chapter can be summarised as follows:

(1) The availability of Community funds is an opportunity for innovative businesses to obtain funds for further research.

(2) Those funds obviously provide opportunities in turn for consultants with relevant skills, who will also now find it easier to establish themselves in other countries of the EEC.

(3) Subject to the competition rules, small or medium-sized businesses could cooperate in joint ventures.

(4) It is of course possible to acquire, take over, or merge with, existing businesses in other European countries, but this requires a lot of patience. It is essential to build up a strong team of professionals so that the complicated formalities are complied with.

(5) Part of the strategy could be to acquire, merge with, or take over another company in the UK. This may enable a business to have a strong base or to be involved with a business already exporting to other countries of the Community. Again it is essential to have a strong team of professionals.

PART 2
Practical considerations

CHAPTER 5
Product safety and specifications

5.1 Introduction

There can only be a Single Market in the European Community if the laws regulating trading in the Member States are at least approximately the same. To this end the Commission has produced various directives, and some agreement has been reached in relation to product safety and specifications.

There are still, however, some important differences, so the purpose of this chapter is to highlight both these and the similarities. Businesses will need to know about such matters as part of their plans for expansion into other countries of the EEC.

5.2 The Civil Judgments and Jurisdiction Act 1982

5.2.1 The European framework

The Brussels Convention on Jurisdiction and the Enforcement of Judgments on Civil and Commercial Matters of 1968 has the aim of harmonising the rules in respect of the recognition of judgments throughout the Community. Subject to a few safeguards the courts in one country should in general recognise the judgments of the courts in another. It has taken some time for this idea to become adopted as law, and it is still not in force throughout the Community.

In the UK it has been given effect through the Civil Judgments and Jurisdiction Act 1982, and the provisions of the Convention were brought into force with effect from 1 January 1987. It initially only applies to a few countries.

5.2.2 The principles

A judgment in the law court of another Convention country can be enforced in the English courts subject to some exceptions. A list of the main principles affecting business law is given below:

(1) 'A judgment given in a contracting state shall be recognised by the other contracting states without any special procedure being required' (Article 26 of the Convention).

(2) There are some exceptions such as public policy (Article 27) or where the judgment is irreconcilable with another in the state in which recognition is being sought (Article 28). Article 27(2) adds that a judgment need not be recognised where the original judgment was made when the defendant failed to appear and had not been served with the documents, etc. to give him or her sufficient time to prepare a defence.

(3) A judgment may be stayed if an appeal is pending (Article 30).

(4) An action in contract may be brought in the courts of the place of the performance of the obligation in question (Article 5). The parties to the contract can, however, displace this rule by agreeing to the submission of disputes to a court in another Convention country (Article 17). The exception does not apply to consumer or certain insurance contracts.

(5) An action in tort may be brought in the country where the damage occurred (Article 5).

5.3	**Product liability**

5.3.1 The Consumer Protection Act 1987 – general safety requirement

Section 10 of the Consumer Protection Act 1987 makes it a criminal offence to supply, offer or agree to supply, or expose or possess for supply, consumer goods which fail to comply with the general safety requirement. That requirement is defined by reference to some general definitions as well as to published standards of safety including those issued by the Commission. Community law therefore affects businesses in the UK.

Those general safety requirements include the purposes for which the goods are being marketed, their get-up, any trade mark, instructions or warnings given, or which would be given, with respect to the keeping, use or consumption of the goods. Another consideration is the 'existence of any means by which it would have been reasonable (taking into account the cost, likelihood and extent of any improvement) for the goods to have been made safer' (s 10(2)(b) Consumer Protection Act 1987).

An illustration of how this might operate is found in the case *Associated Dairies v Hartley* [1979] IRLR 171. This related to precautions judged in the light of 'reasonable practicability' under the Health and Safety at Work etc. Act 1974. The employer was allowed to continue its practice of allowing employees to buy safety shoes on no interest credit terms. The alternative where the shoes would have been provided free of charge would have been far too expensive for that employer.

The duty in relation to section 10 is certainly not a high one because it only requires compliance with the relevant Community obligation or other enactment. Any failure to do more is not an offence under the Act.

There are some defences, such as that the goods were not to be supplied as new goods to specific people, and that retailers reasonably believed the safety standards had been observed. Reasonable belief that the goods would not be used or consumed within the United Kingdom is also a defence to a prosecution under the Act.

A company could therefore produce goods not in compliance with a Community standard and export them to another country in the EEC yet not commit an offence under section 10. The law of that country, however, will then take over, and penalise the importer or distributor.

In the UK there are penalties other than fines for contravening this part of the Consumer Protection Act 1987. These include:

(a) forfeiture of the offending goods,

(b) prohibition notices preventing dealing in them,

(c) notices to warn – requiring a warning to be included with goods considered by the Secretary of State to be unsafe,

(d) suspension notices preventing any dealings with the goods.

The moral of all this is that all businesses must comply with Community regulations. Manufacturers and importers of goods for export or re-export will have to keep up to date as noted below.

5.3.2 Standards

The Common Market is eliminating technical barriers in three different ways:

(1) Member States have to notify the Commission of any proposed national technical regulations under the terms of Directive 83/189.

(2) The European Standardisation Committee and the European Standardisation Committee for Electrical Products are drawing up directives, some of which are noted below. These two bodies are known as CEN (*Comité Européen Normalisation*) and CENELEC (*Comité Européen Normalisation Electrotechnique*) respectively.

(3) The Commission is working on setting up har-

monised standards in relation to testing and certification, while some countries such as the UK and France are collaborating in this area.

Directives have already been laid down in relation to simple pressure vessels and toy safety. Various topics are now being discussed such as construction products, personal protection equipment, machinery safety, electromagnetic compatibility, measuring instruments, medical devices and certain non-industrial gas appliances or those with a water temperature above 105°C.

Food law has been considerably affected by directives covering certain food additives, materials and articles in contact with food (79/112), sampling and analysis (85/591), and the composition of certain foods. There are considerable projected changes in this area, including additives, irradiation, nutrition, labelling and many more. On a similar topic much work is being done on public health and hygiene standards.

5.3.3 Keeping up to date

In the light of the Consumer Protection Act 1987 and the EEC directives mentioned in *5.3.1* and *5.3.2* above, businesses which distribute products either in the UK alone or across the frontier into other EEC countries need to keep up to date with the latest standards. This can be achieved in various ways:

(1) membership of the appropriate trade association, which keeps members up to date with the latest developments,

(2) subscription to the appropriate technical computer data bases,

(3) membership of the British Standards Institution. This provides members with up-to-date information about the changes, and also has other services such as a data base and marketing information. It can also help with information about overseas standards. A small business would find the inexpensive member-

ship fee an entry into those services which a large company has in-house, and enable it to compete more effectively in the international market.

5.4 Consumer safety

5.4.1 Consumer Protection Act 1987 and defective products

As a result of Directive 85/374/EEC the UK government introduced the Consumer Protection Act 1987 as part of the process to harmonise EEC trading laws. It has not succeeded in this objective, because each country has been allowed to take one of two courses of action.

The UK Act in accordance with the Directive insists that manufacturers and importers of goods into the EEC are liable for defects in products causing death or personal injury to consumers or causing loss or damage to any property including land (s 5).

That property must be intended for private use or consumption, which could cause problems in definition. Some computers, although ordinarily designed mainly for playing games, can be used for business. It is difficult to see where the cheap IBM clones fit in.

Liability can be extended to retailers who do not disclose their supplier of any defective product.

5.4.2 Defences

There are of course defences to an action under the first part of the Consumer Protection Act 1987, and a lot of these are related to time. An action, in general terms, may not be brought more than the end of the third year after the damage became observable (s 11A(4) & (5) Limitation Act 1980). The amended Limitation Act allows extensions of time under limited circumstances (s 33 gives the court a discretion to extend the limit depending on 'the circumstances of the case') subject to an absolute time bar of the end of the tenth year (s 11A(3)).

There is another defence known as 'state of the art'

under section 4(1)(e) of the Consumer Protection Act 1987. This is best illustrated by a law case *Roe v Minister of Health* [1954] 2 QB 66. An anaesthetist administered a spinal anaesthetic from a glass ampoule, which had itself been kept in a solution of phenol. Unbeknown to anyone at the time the solution seeped through minute cracks in the glass and contaminated the anaesthetic, so that the patient was paralysed from the waist downwards.

Four years later in 1951 the scientists woke up to the fact that minute cracks like this could occur. The answer to the problem was simple – a purple dye was added to the phenol, so any leakage through the ampoule would be obvious.

The unfortunate patient sued for some recompense for his terrible injuries, but the judges refused to hold the health authority responsible. The 'state of the art' or the state of knowledge in 1947 was such that the danger was not known.

5.4.3 Consumer protection – no harmonisation in the EEC

A consumer would normally only have to prove that there was a defect, that it caused the damage, and the action is being brought within the time limits. In the previous paragraph it was noted that a defence to a claim by a consumer for such damages is that scientific knowledge could not have discovered the defect.

The EEC Directive 85/374/EEC allows this defence but also permits countries to disallow it. This is important to those businesses selling goods into, say, France, where this concept of strict liability applies. The answer is adequate product liability insurance, and insurers or brokers must be kept constantly updated about the markets in which products are being sold. Insurance premiums or excesses may go up, if experience is ultimately found to be bad, but this is better than a rejected claim because someone forgot to tell the insurers what was going on.

Anyone who distributes goods purely in the UK has no reason to be complacent because of the Civil Judgments and Jurisdiction Act 1982 mentioned in *5.2.1*. Actions in tort can be brought in the country where the damage occurs. A buyer could, say, buy a product from an Oxford Street store in London, but take it home with him or her to France. If the product is defective, the manufacturer or importer into the EEC will be strictly liable for the damage caused by the defect. It will not be allowed the defence of 'state of the art', and all things being equal an English court will enforce the judgment of the French judges. Businesses in this position should check that their insurance cover is adequate.

5.5 | Product liability – action for businesses

(1) Companies which are actively looking to increase their market in the EEC must keep up to date with the coming changes affecting standards. At the same time it is obvious that complete harmonisation of standards will not happen until long after 1992. Membership of trade bodies or the British Standards Institution gives access to the latest standards as well as to information about markets.

(2) Laws relating to product liability to consumers are also going to differ for some time to come, although there are complaints that the UK has not fulfilled its obligations required by the EEC Directive 85/374/EEC. The result at the moment is strict liability in some countries but not in others. Insurers and brokers must be kept up to date with the business's products and markets, and the adequacy of liability cover must be regularly reviewed.

CHAPTER 6
Logistics

6.1	Definitions

This chapter will highlight certain aspects of logistics, which is the currently popular word to describe the process of a business from the obtaining of any goods or services to the supply of the end product. It is therefore also called the supply chain – an important part of a business's activities.

Michael Porter in his book *Competitive Advantage* suggested that there were two aspects as follows:

Inbound logistics such as receiving, storing and disseminating inputs to the product. Examples are materials' handling, warehousing, inventory control, vehicle scheduling and returns to suppliers.

Outbound logistics are concerned with the collection, storage and distribution of the final product to customers. They include warehousing of the finished goods, materials' handling, delivery vehicle operation, order processing and scheduling.

Companies which are expanding their activities through exporting or the appointment of distributors or agents will have to examine their procedures in relation to outbound logistics. Businesses which are setting up branches in other countries will be have to review inbound logistics as well.

It is an important area, which requires careful planning. There are changes in relation to transport such as the Channel Tunnel, while computer-based systems can help in the more efficient handling of goods.

As if to emphasise all this the Institute of Purchasing and Supply has brought out its own publication, *Logistics*, and appointed a Head of Logistics. It is adding subjects to its syllabus and training courses.

Another important factor is that of cost. According to the AT Kearney survey of 1987, logistic costs averaged 21% of value added for European firms, whereas in 1981 the figure was 11%. This may be an indication of inefficiency, but companies such as BMW have changed their logistic structure to make it more efficient.

Businesses which are expanding their activities into other countries must analyse this area very carefully, and try to get it right from the outset. It can make them more competitive.

6.2 | Exporting

Some companies will not actually move their base overseas but will expand by means of direct exports or sales through distributors or agents. They will therefore have to take action including the following:

(1) the appointment of a forwarding agent who will arrange the transportation of goods and the associated paperwork,

(2) a review of internal warehouse procedures to ensure that they are efficient and cost-effective,

(3) a review of purchasing procedures to ensure that they are both efficient and that the right materials to suit local needs have been obtained,

(4) a review of the packaging needed (including instruction books in the appropriate languages),

(5) pricing policy in relation both to cost savings as a result of the review and to any extra overheads.

6.3 | Transporting goods across European frontiers

Some businesses will be able to use their own resources to transport goods, and the process is being made easier. The principle is laid down in Title IV in the EEC Treaty, where the objective is a 'common transport policy'.

Achievements so far include the Single Administrative Document, which has replaced a total of approximately 100 forms. This makes it easier to take goods, including samples for trade exhibitions, across frontiers within the Community.

There is still a long way to go, because some countries still operate a permit system in relation to the transport of goods by road hauliers. This is due to end by 1992.

There are also other practical points to consider. Most of Europe uses a 1,000 × 800 pallet, but the UK specification is 1,000 × 1,200. Some people will remember the fuss, when it was suggested that lorries of 40 tonnes gross should be allowed on the roads. That is the weight in most of Europe (in some countries 44 tonnes is allowed) but the UK compromised on 38 tonnes.

Businesses which intend to transport their own goods across frontiers must therefore:

(1) review the paperwork procedures in relation to the transportation of the particular goods,

(2) take the action recommended in points (2) to (5) in 6.2 above.

6.4 | Small deliveries

Small deliveries can of course be sent in the post, but more urgent or precious items where a guaranteed delivery is required can be despatched by:

(1) a courier firm,

(2) one of the special services offered by the Post Office such as Datapost or Superservice.

6.5 | Overseas warehouses

6.5.1 Basic considerations

Some businesses will need to set up their own distribution centres in order to service their customers or their own branches. Location of the warehouse will depend on where those customers or branches are themselves to be found, the availability of the necessary roads, rail or other transport facilities and of course the resources, such as the budget for rent, available to the enterprise. Points (2) to (5) in 6.2 above must also be part of the action plan.

Once the details as to the property have been settled, a warehouse plan has to be decided, and it should include the following:

(1) number and type of personnel,
(2) vehicles required,
(3) storage and materials handling systems needed (fork-lift trucks, conveyor belts, etc.),
(4) computerisation (see 6.7 below),
(5) administration generally,
(6) systems monitoring,
(7) packing equipment and materials needed.

6.5.2 Dynamic solutions

The setting up of an overseas network of warehouses can be expensive, but modern technology can help to control the cost. The NFC Consulting Group reports in *The NFC Contract Distribution Report 1989* that it has developed two alternatives to overcome the cost disadvantages of running several small warehouses.

The business sets up two dual units which may be several hundreds of miles apart, but it sets up a single administrative system. The traditional method is to consider all the warehouses as separate units servicing different areas with fixed boundaries.

The Dynamic Sourcing approach is to treat such boundaries as flexible depending on the workload. Deliveries from one warehouse may cover a large area on one day, while the other has the same amount of work over a smaller district. On the following day the situation may be reversed.

This system is backed up by Dynamic Channel Selection which works out the best way to utilise each warehouse's transport facilities. Small inefficient loads may be sent by means of local contractors.

6.6 Alternatives to the use of own transport or overseas warehouses

6.6.1 Contractors

To set up warehouses or a transportation system is obviously expensive and takes a lot of resources. An alternative is to appoint contractors to do the work, but it is essential to choose the right one. A check list should include the following:

(1) Is the contractor financially sound? (references should be obtained – for general principles see *3.3.6*).

(2) Does the contractor have sufficient delivery facilities in the area to be covered?

(3) References should be obtained from existing customers.

(4) If there are any special requirements (such as refrigerated vans) does the contractor have adequate vehicles?

(5) Does the contractor have an adequate record keeping system to trace deliveries? (this is particularly important if the recall of a defective product has to be arranged).

(6) If the contractor is to supply warehouse facilities, are they adequate and efficient?

(7) If the contractor is based overseas, will there be any language difficulties?

(8) Does the contractor have an adequate problem solving service?

6.6.2 Shared distribution services

Some companies which already distribute their own products offer their own transport facilities for hire. A check list as in *6.6.1* should be drawn up.

6.7 Computer Integrated Logistics

Although more detail about computers is contained in chapter 10, they can be used to make the whole system more efficient in the following ways:

(1) programs to monitor the transport fleet,

(2) programs to monitor or control the warehouse operation,

(3) programs to assist in buying and the control of stocks.

6.8 Logistics – an opportunity

Expansion into Europe is therefore an opportunity for businesses to review their logistics generally. It can be a large part of their budgets, yet the use of modern technology can result in savings and further benefits such as increased profitability. A further check list will be found in chapter 2.

CHAPTER 7
Standards for manufacturers, importers and distributors

7.1	**Introduction**

There can be no Single Market if each country has differing technical standards. At the moment, for example, there is BSI in the UK, DIN in West Germany and AFNOR in France. Change is already on its way in that directives are already being issued to harmonise standards in respect of specific products.

Directives are already agreed in relation to simple pressure vessels and toy safety, and other important ones are under discussion. These include construction products, where the intention is to list essential requirements with which the product has to comply. Such an approach is being used in respect of machinery safety and personal protective equipment.

From this it seems that BSI and other national standards will have an important part to play. They should all be roughly the same, because they will have to incorporate the directives worked out by CEN or CENELEC. Any product which complies with the Community requirements will be able to carry an EC mark, so they can then be circulated freely throughout Member States.

This is all very well, but the work is just beginning. It will be a long time, probably after 1992, that anything will be done about differing electrical standards in the various countries. For the time being the UK will retain its square pin plugs and internal fuses, rarely changed by the consumer from 13 amps to one appropriate for the electrical equipment it serves, while over the Channel there are round pins – and these are not all exactly the same! When the time comes for change there will be arguments as to which is the best system.

In the meantime businesses will have to deal with differing standards, and will have to find ways to revise their products in accordance with the relevant requirements. In this chapter there are examples taken from the high-tech world of computing of how to develop a policy in relation to standards. Although this is obviously relevant to that industry, other businesses can learn from this experience, and tailor their own strategy for business expansion.

7.2 Where to find the information

In order to remain competitive businesses will have to be up to date with all the changes that are coming. There are several possible ways by which this can be done:

(1) Council directives are published in the Official Journal of the European Communities, but because this contains a lot of information smaller enterprises will not want to take out a subscription.

(2) The Department of Trade and Industry can often help with answers to specific enquiries.

(3) Membership of the British Standards Institution (the BSI) is a useful way of keeping up to date. In addition to its publications containing information about the UK standards, there are others such as the *Overseas Standards Updating Service* with its monthly updates on pre-listed national and foreign standards publications. Better still, members can subscribe to a scheme whereby they automatically receive details about amendments to the relevant standards. There is also an enquiry service and a computer data base which can be accessed by members who have the right computer equipment. Another benefit is the Institution's *Technical Help to Exporters*.

(4) Most industries have their own trade associations, which obviously can help with information of direct relevance to members. Addresses of some of these will be found in Appendix 1. Some organisations will already have Community and other contacts, which will have uses besides those relating to EEC directives. It is obvious that harmonisation of technical standards will not have been completed by the end of 1992, but some industries will be able to create their own. Examples in the computer world are noted in 7.3 below.

(5) Some technical and educational bodies have computer data bases which can be accessed by subscribers.

There is another important advantage of membership of the BSI or a trade association, in that members can influence policy. The BSI, for example, is represented on CEN and CENELEC in the Community, which are working to harmonise European standards. The December 1988 issue of *BSI News* appealed to readers to help the BSI to get its planning right for 1992 and beyond by letting the Institution have their views. It also publishes draft BSI standards so that people can comment on them.

Businesses for which compliance with technical standards are important should therefore join a trade association or the BSI or both, in order to keep informed of what is happening and to influence events.

7.3 International technical standards

Companies, such as Prime Computer, have answered the questions posed by the need to comply with varying standards in various ways:

(1) Companies providing products for the international market have of course to look at what is happening throughout the world. They therefore have to make products complying with international as well as national standards. The groups involved

in forming the International Organisation for Standardisation (ISO) include:

> BSI – British Standards Institution
>
> ECMA – European Computer Manufacturers Association
>
> IEEE – Institute of Electrical and Electronic Engineers
>
> NBS – National Bureau of Standards
>
> ANSI – American National Standards Institute
>
> CCITT – International Telephone and Telegraph Consultative Committee

(2) Prime Computer, for example, has manufacturing facilities in Ireland, so has obtained the Irish Quality Mark and is attaining approval to the ISO DIS-9004.

(3) Its Customer Service Division in the UK is working with the BSI to obtain certification to the standard BS5750 Part 1 1987/ISO 9001 (Doc QAS 3302/187).

(4) Anyone who has used a computer will be aware that one of the components that make it work is the operating system. Prime Computer, for example, has its own operating system, but also supplies products conforming, for example, to version V of AT&T's version of Unix. Similar considerations apply to computer programming languages, standards for CAD/CAM (Computer Aided Design/Computer Aided Manufacturing) and data exchange including the European VDA standard.

(5) Companies which have computers in different countries often want to network them so that data can be transferred or interchanged. Some companies like Prime Computer therefore are committed to the Open Systems Interconnection reference model and to the national and international standards that operate within it.

(6) Companies obviously wish to supply government

departments, so in the computing world they have to monitor Government OSI Profiles (GOSIP).

7.4 | European standards – a case study

Although there are international standards, there are national technical differences. The aim in the Community is to harmonise them by means of directives issued through the Joint European Standards Institution, CEN and CENELEC. There are also problems much greater than the different types of electrical plugs used in the various Member States. Telecommunications standards differ, and this can cause technical problems for those not prepared for them.

Prime Computer has dealt with such issues as follows:

(1) It has adopted a standard called X.400 as the main protocol for electronic message exchange, and will ensure that it will comply with, among others, the standards produced by CEN/CENELEC.

(2) Prime Computer is a member of EurOSInet, which has been formed by computer systems and services suppliers for systems networking in Europe. They have produced their own *Outline Charter and Code of Practice.* The intention of the organisation is 'to increase market awareness and confidence in OSI as a practical guide to problems of systems inter-working'.

(3) Prime Computer is also a member of the European MAP (Manufacturing Automation Protocol) User Group (EMUG) whose intentions include: 'To harmonise European efforts into a single coherent strategy for influencing development of an international standard set of communication specifications using MAP as a baseline'.

7.5 User groups

An aspect of both technical standards and marketing is to know the market, and one method is to join user groups to find out what potential and actual customers are thinking. In the computing world there is the European MAP User Group, one of whose objectives is 'To promote a full appreciation of the advances of MAP for European users and vendors'. The Corporation for Open Systems holds user group meetings and workshops on standards.

7.6 Promoting standards

It is sometimes in the interests of particular industries to promote standards if none already exists. Businesses could therefore make a joint approach to the British Standards Institution to promote their own ideas. Grundmann (UK) Limited has investigated this policy, and was told that this process could take four or five years.

7.7 Watch out for differences

Although efforts are being made to harmonise standards, many differences remain. These are not just in the area of manufactured goods.

An example of this was contained in the report by the Consumers' Association *Holiday Which?* in January 1989. Although hotels in Benidorm complied with local safety regulations, the report stated that 'having unprotected stairways flouts every accepted fire safety code. It ignores the lessons from past fires which show them to be the major culprit in fire deaths'.

Factories too could be a problem. The author once visited an Italian factory which manufactured latex-based products, some of which were inflammable. There was a brightly burning bonfire within the factory gates, while also inside the factory yard was a building containing both flats and the factory boiler room – a potentially lethal mixture, although someone must have approved the arrangement.

Compliance with local standards therefore may not be enough, and consideration must be given to wider issues such as those of health and safety.

7.8 | Practical conclusions

From these practical examples a business expanding its activities overseas should consider the following steps in relation to its compliance with, and ascertainment of, standards:

(1) Membership of bodies such as the BSI, which can provide information through its services to members in the area of standards and advice generally. It also provides the opportunity to influence policy, although the process of promoting new standards can be a slow one.

(2) Membership of trade bodies which can also provide information and influence policy. Computer manufacturers are, for example, promoting international industry standards outside the official organisations such as the BSI and CEN/CENELEC to the advantage of manufacturers, distributors and end users.

(3) Membership of user groups which can supply feedback about reactions to standards, products, service and the like. This can also be useful in framing the company's marketing policy.

(4) All standards should be reviewed in the light of other requirements such as that of health and safety. General Common Market standards should be drafted with these in mind, but harmonisation has only just started and local regulations may not be stringent enough.

CHAPTER 8
Personnel

8.1 | ## Introduction

A key factor in any plan for business expansion is personnel. As well as any policy about the jobs to be created, there are other considerations. A Trade Union view from Peter Coldrick in 8.8 below shows that working conditions are not the same throughout the Community. Even more than that there are cultural differences which affect the way people work. These have important implications for those companies which are opening overseas branches or subsidiaries.

8.2 | ## Mobility of labour

8.2.1 Opportunities for UK workers abroad

Article 48 of the EEC Treaty guarantees 'freedom of movement for workers', and this could have the following effects:

(1) Manpower, the employment specialist, feels that this is unlikely to affect lower paid unskilled workers very much, as for this group there will be no particular benefits, such as higher pay or employment prospects, to tempt them away, when items such as the cost of living and travel are taken into account.

(2) There will obviously be greater opportunities for skilled workers, and UK businesses will also be sending out their own staff to run or monitor the progress of their new branches or subsidiaries.

(3) One obstacle to the free movement of workers from the UK is the lack of language ability. It is generally impossible to use people with higher

qualifications in languages, because they have been taught in such an academic way. What is needed, for example, is people with a knowledge of commercial French. Their counterparts in, say France and Germany, do not have this deficiency in relation to English and other languages they may learn. The CBI is doing a lot to publicise in industry, commerce and schools the need for such a practical basis behind the learning of languages.

8.2.2 Solving the skills shortage

The newspapers from time to time report that British industry is unable to recruit sufficient skilled staff, but the Single Market can provide some solutions. There is, for example, a pool of skilled engineers in West Germany. Manpower points out that it and other agencies in the same position will probably be able to assist UK businesses and to fulfil those demands.

Training local staff is of course another solution as noted in 8.7 below.

8.3 Forming a strategy

One way of finding out about conditions abroad is to go there and contact local lawyers and employment agencies. Another means, as part of the research into this aspect of business expansion, may therefore be made easier by a telephone call to the local branch of an employment agency. That branch will of course be unlikely to have the information itself, but may be part of an organisation which does.

8.4 Following up the strategy in a different culture

Once the expanding business has decided on its strategy, it has to establish personnel procedures for its new branch or subsidiary. It may also have to send over its own executives either to set up a new organisation, or it may have to take over an existing one. Those executives will usually find a very different working atmosphere or culture than in the UK.

The author has, for example, been involved in the Dutch subsidiary of a UK company and worked in a UK subsidiary of a Dutch company. By UK standards the Dutch style of management is more autocratic, and there is a great emphasis on skills measurement. People from this country may find this difficult to get used to, but they should remember that it has produced some very successful businesses.

Manpower feels that the function of international employment agencies is to understand these cultural barriers, and to equip managers and staff to overcome them. Qualifications and standards for office staff should have similar meaning throughout the Community. Any company opening for business overseas should therefore take the following points into their business plan:

(1) There are obviously differences in employment law as mentioned in 8.1 above.

(2) The cultural differences have just been mentioned.

(3) Staff in the parent company will need training relevant to the new situation. UK staff going abroad in particular may need help in learning a new language or bringing their existing knowledge up to an acceptable standard. Manpower particularly emphasise that individuals must be multi-faceted to work successfully in an international environment. They must, for example, be prepared for any cultural differences, as otherwise they will not be able to cope.

(4) There must be a consistency of skill throughout the enlarged organisation, so a training or a retraining programme and the setting of standards and quality control must have a high priority. The whole world is changing and in the international company information technology and electronic communica-

tions are having a greater impact. Some Community countries are ahead of the UK in this respect, while others are behind. People must learn about, and be able to use where necessary, the new technology.

(5) Such training is all part of the objective of setting clear objectives to staff.

(6) Skills measurement mentioned in more detail in 8.5 below is an important means of setting standards and attaining consistency throughout the business. In some countries employees expect it, and Manpower take the view that managers in the UK have to become more accustomed to using professional methods of skills measurement.

8.5 | Setting standards and measuring skills

8.5.1 Methods

As mentioned in 8.4 there are various methods of obtaining consistency, which include setting standards and skills measurement. Employers and employees consider these to be very important in some countries, and in any event they can be used effectively in what is known as 'managing human resources'. They need not result in rigid relationships between employers and employees, which is sometimes used as an excuse by smaller enterprises not to do anything at all. This can cause its own problems, particularly where an employee seems determined to be difficult.

This section of the book therefore outlines two of the techniques in setting standards and managing skills, which a business expanding overseas will have to use.

8.5.2 The job description or specification

It helps if employees know what they have to do, and, although training is part of the process, a job specification can help both employer and employee in setting objectives. A typical job description could include:

(1) job title,

(2) a brief description of the job,

(3) to whom the employee reports,

(4) those reporting to the employee,

(5) contacts outside the business,

(6) major responsibilities,

(7) duties including a description of equipment used,

(8) hours of work,

(9) style of dress (if this is important or relevant to the job).

A job description is a recruitment tool, in that from it the employer can judge what qualifications and type of person is needed, but some businesses comment that it is too inflexible. The smaller company needs people who respond quickly to a quickly changing business situation.

The answer is that the job description can include a statement to that effect, e.g.: 'Because the company does not employ many people, all employees must be flexible and be prepared to undertake tasks reasonably within their capabilities'.

8.5.3 Terms of employment

Because each country has different laws relating to employment, it is only possible to mention some general principles in relation to setting standards. In the UK, for example, employers have to specify any relevant disciplinary rules and procedures (s 1(4) Employment Protection (Consolidation) Act 1978), and this is obviously good practice anyway.

To this should be added any health and safety rules. One company will dismiss any employee who carries matches, lighters, calculators and the like into certain high risk areas of the plant. Although this is the negative aspect of setting goals, such important rules must be made clear at the outset.

8.5.4 Appraisal

Employees also expect regular pay reviews, so this can be used as an opportunity to see whether or not standards are being maintained. Managers can set standards and find out any career objectives or training needs. All this will be the result of the staff appraisal which, as noted in 8.4 above, is regarded as important by many enterprises on continental Europe but also by many in the UK.

The aim is to move away from a subjective feeling that 'so-and-so is a good chap' or that 'I find so-and-so very irritating', towards a more objective judgment. The person conducting the review or appraisal is forced to consider each aspect of the employee's work to come to a final conclusion.

The appraisal is furthermore discussed with the employee, so that goals can be set. It can be very positive, but managers may have to be trained to use it effectively. Appraisal forms will obviously differ for each business, but an example of what they may contain is as follows:

Name   Department

Date of joining the company

Job title   Since

Each question should be graded from 1 to 5 as follows:
1. Excellent 2. Very good 3. Satisfactory 4. Not up to standard 5. Very poor

1. The Appraisal
(a) Knowledge of the employee's specific job
(b) Knowledge of the department's objectives
(c) Accuracy
(d) Speed
(e) Cooperation with colleagues within the department
(f) Cooperation with other colleagues
(g) Initiative
(h) Time keeping
(i) Sickness record
(j) Initiative

2. Promotional potential

Reasons

3. What are any training needs?

4. Specific reasons for any of the grades in the Appraisal

5. Future objectives for the employee

Sections 1 to 5 completed by: (date)

6. Employees comments, signature and date

7. Comments of manager interviewing the employee

Section 7 completed by: (date)

8.6   Public relations

One aspect of expanding a business that can be neglected is that of public relations in the area of management and employee relations. It all is part of setting objectives, and of making employees feel that they are part of a team.

One method is the newsletter which, in addition to containing the usual news about employees' achievements and happy events, can get across the management's objectives. Some companies issue their annual accounts with a commentary in the form of diagrams and charts.

It has to be done well, as otherwise a company newsletter will be regarded as a propaganda sheet. If there are no in-house skills, a public relations firm could be given the job. Many of them already have experience in this field and, of course, the final result will have to be translated into the relevant languages. Printing in this modern age is not a problem as a result of computerised desktop publishing, but it is a job for professionals.

8.7   Training

Staff must of course be trained, but a programme should include the encouragement of continuing professional education for appropriate employees. This might be encouraged by the Community itself by restricting the use of some professional descriptions, such as accountant, to those people holding qualifications meeting its definition of a higher education diploma. It may also insist that to retain their professional description people will be expected to attend continuing professional education seminars in order to gain sufficient credits.

The professional bodies, such as the Institute of Financial Accountants, are taking this very seriously. That Institute, for example, is already organising a series of professional education seminars linked to its own examination syllabus, which is designed to help up-date skills. The courses will be open to people who are not members of the Institute, and can also be adapted to a system of credits, if the Community should require it.

Those who direct and manage businesses also need training on how to prepare for 1992, and the Confederation of British Industry (CBI) Initiative is very welcome. It includes conferences, courses and roadshows as part of a drive to help British industry prepare for 1992.

8.8 | The Trade Union view

Trade Unions also regard the Single Market in Europe as an opportunity. David Lea, TUC Assistant General Secretary, wrote in *Modern Management* Autumn 1988, 'Workers' rights in Britain are in many respects less favourable than in the rest of Europe, a point to which we will be drawing attention at every opportunity, because there is a good deal of mythology to the contrary'. Peter Coldrick, Secretary of the European Trade Union Confederation, in the Autumn 1987 issue of *Modern Management* affirmed, 'The ETUC certainly has not given up its belief that European legislation in certain areas is required – for instance we still strongly support the draft Vredeling Directive regarding workers' information and consultation in MNCs – and indeed we believe that the reforms to the Treaty of Rome made by the single Act will make such legislation easier to adopt. However, we are also realists and we know that building Europe and making it into a true multi-faceted Community is bound to be a long task. Neither the employers nor most of our members want to sign binding European-wide collective agreements to-morrow, but for our part we believe that the social dialogue can be a foundation on which can be patiently built, a European system of industrial relations. What its precise future shape will be we do not know, but a start has been made.'

8.9 The key to successful expansion

Although industrial robots and computers have taken away much repetitive work, they have not replaced people on which the success of any business expansion depends. The elements of that success are:

(1) the involvement of the professionals in establishing a staff policy,

(2) the establishment of personnel procedures to motivate and monitor employees' activities,

(3) communication to employees of the overall objectives of the enterprise,

(4) the establishment of training procedures and the encouragement of appropriate staff to participate in the continuing education programmes of the professional bodies,

(5) staff relations may require negotiations with Trade Unions.

CHAPTER 9
Computers

Planning for computers

A business expanding its activities overseas, if it does not have computerised systems for such activities as accounting or word processing, should consider installing computers. If this is done correctly they can provide lots of benefits, but otherwise there can be some problems adversely affecting the efficiency of the business – what in 1975 the Polish legal periodical *Prawo i Zycie* – 'Law and Life' – called the 'Criminality of the Computer'.

In order to avoid such problems the time to start planning is now. The author was once asked to change the paperwork and procedures relating to the processing of orders in a small distribution company. Although this was not in the brief, future computerisation was anticipated, so the system was designed with that in mind. When a computer was introduced just over a year later, none of the new procedures nor the basic paperwork had to be changed.

Using computers in Europe

Computers can be used to make a business more efficient in many ways including the following:

(1) Accounts – Although the various branches may keep their own accounting records, a company will normally consolidate all the figures into a set of management accounts. This can be achieved by means of computer accounting programs with multi-currency facilities. As an alternative some accountancy programs allow the user to transfer data into a spreadsheet, and the figures can be consolidated there.

(2) Spreadsheets – These are particularly useful for the analysis of figures, but note that a data disk of the French version of a program will probably not run with an English version of the program.

(3) Data bases – These can be used to keep various types of record including customer records, which can then be merged into a suitable word processing program in order to send out standard letters.

(4) Word processing – This should improve the efficiency and quality of typing. Standard letters and contracts can be kept on file and called up when needed. A related facility is desktop publishing but this should only be used by people experienced in layouts, etc.

(5) CAD and CAM – These systems can make the drawing office much more efficient.

(6) Networking – This is a means of linking computers together, and certainly where a company is of a reasonable size, it can improve communications with overseas branches. Mail can be sent electronically between those branches, and bulletin boards can be used as an aid to problem solving. An employee in one branch who cannot find a solution to a technical problem can send out a request for advice to all the other branches. The January 1988 issue of *Importing Today* reported that Emery Worldwide had installed EMCOM, a name for its Emery Control Communications Network. It was therefore able to track shipments for all its customers, and provide information to enquirers quickly.

(7) External data bases – As has already been mentioned, subscribers to information data bases can use the computer to obtain access to them.

9.3 A computer strategy

For UK's Computacenter the following elements are an essential part of any computer strategy:

(1) It is essential to choose and consult an expert supplier at an early stage, so that it can get involved with all the projects and help with planning the right strategy.

(2) A company expanding into another European country needs a dealer who has contacts and some leverage there. Computacenter is based in the UK, but recognises the international nature of modern business. Because of its standing as a leading IBM distributor in the UK, and a winner of the IBM United Kingdom Quality Dealer of the Year Award, it has therefore built up strong relationships with other reputable dealers throughout Europe. This provides the benefit of a consistent approach.

(3) Once a strategy has been agreed, the detail has then to be worked out. Computacenter solves this by having experts divisions such as Software or CAD/CAM, because it is important to have the back-up of people who are experts in the relevant areas. No CAD system will be sold without training.

(4) Another reason for obtaining the help of a dealer with general European experience is that there can be buying advantages.

(5) Anyone who uses computers knows that things will go wrong. The supplier must be able to provide after-sales support. In line with its view that after-sales service is preparatory work for future business, Computacenter provides various kinds of help. This includes a hot-line service, because many problems can be solved over the telephone. In the UK it can also offer a two-hour call out, 24 hours a day, 365 days a year, and claims to achieve it.

(6) Training is an essential part of the strategy, and Computacenter provides courses on how to use popular software for absolute beginners to those who want special customised programmes. It has a consistent approach at all its training centres.

It is therefore possible to plan a computer strategy

from the UK for a company with branches in other European countries. That is because the plan will usually be conceived and controlled from the UK head office. The strategy is essential to ensure the efficient use of the various computers.

In those circumstances the person responsible for the plan will have to involve a dealer or consultant. That dealer or consultant must have European experience and sufficient resources for the task.

9.4 Saving a computer system from disaster – a case study

The author once had to set up a multi-currency computerised accounting system and save it from disaster:

(1) The company had a stand-alone Personal Computer and an accounts program capable of recording the transactions of the UK head office and the US branches. No proper accounting records had been kept for four months save for manual cash books. Payments received against invoices were merely noted on the documents themselves, and a similar primitive procedure was adopted for accounts payable.

(2) The computer program had fortunately been installed, and it was decided to use the same ledger and account numbers already set up. The system was not ideal, and if there had been more time all this would have been changed.

(3) If resources had been unlimited a lot of extra help would have been used, but the company was going through financial difficulties. Only one temporary VDU operator was hired.

(4) The manuals that came with the program were very clear, so they made it easier to design the forms, from which the VDU operator could type the data.

(5) The opening accounts balances were at least available, and these were entered onto the computer with no difficulty.

(6) The customer information was entered onto the sales ledger and the invoice details followed. Similar procedures were adopted for the purchase ledger. Once this had been done, the cash books were entered onto the system.

(7) Because of the haste in which the data was entered onto the system, everyone was informed that the first management accounts would only provide a guide as to the company's performance. Although the system was quite capable of producing the figures, the US$ accounts were set up in the same way as those relating to sterling. All the data could fortunately be transferred to a spreadsheet program, so the accounts were consolidated by means of that.

(8) Although there were mistakes in entering the data, these were usually obvious and were quickly corrected. The shortage of time meant that the entry could not always be controlled by means of batch totals. Despite this the full six months of data was entered in two months, and the final reconciliations to prove the correctness of the exercise took a day.

Computer systems should ideally not have to be installed in such haste, but observance of the basic principles resulted in success. Anyone installing a system or adding to one must:

(1) formulate a detailed plan of how the data is to be entered,

(2) obtain extra help to enter the data – it will usually be needed,

(3) ensure that everyone is trained in the new system,

(4) ensure that the data is entered in a logical and controlled manner,

(5) ensure that the final results are analysed and verified.

9.5 | An aid to sales

Electronic technology could provide different solutions to business expansion. Instead of appointing an agent in another country, the expanding company could employ a salesperson, who would be given a portable computer and a modem compatible with the local telephone system. Every day that salesperson would telephone the UK head office and send information about his or her sales down the telephone lines to the main computer. This would send instructions to the warehouse to send out the goods. Communications can be enhanced by the use of portable fax machines.

The main problem to overcome will be to control the salesperson's activities, and such an employee will have to be a responsible person. More about employment and labour relations is detailed in chapter 8.

9.6 | Computers for business expansion

Computers can be used as a business tool, such as in the area of CAD/CAM, the use of small portable machines to send sales information, or their communications possibilities generally. They are also an important means of making a business more efficient generally through accounts, stock control, word processing or other programs. Software, such as PERT or spreadsheets, can help in the design of the strategy as detailed in chapter 2 for expansion of the business into other countries.

If such strategy includes computers, either as additional equipment or, as a result of a takeover, the absorption of the target business's system into the enlarged enterprise, then the experts must be called in at an early stage. These people must have European experience and contacts, because there are differing communication standards throughout that continent. Adequate after-sales service must be available.

Once the decisions have been taken, the installation

of any new system must be planned carefully. It must include adequate training and an explanation of the system to those staff who are affected by it.

Those businesses whose needs are more modest, in that they only need one or two stand-alone machines still have to follow the basic rules. A computer system can help a business to be more efficient, but if the installation is done badly, that objective can fail with consequent loss of morale by all who are involved.

CHAPTER 10
Finance for expansion

10.1 | Introduction

Most of this chapter has been compiled from information provided by Barclays Bank plc, although the author has added his own impressions and opinions. The section on business plans in particular is based on the author's own experience.

All the banks are, however, taking the advent of the Single European Market seriously, so are making the same or similar preparations as Barclays. This is good news for business customers who wish to expand their activities beyond their own national boundaries. Provided that they have researched their respective projects properly, and their plans are logical they will often find the banks are receptive and more likely to give their support. Such expansion will also be backed up by a range of services to make the running of the expanded international enterprise easier.

All of course will not be sweetness and light, in that some ideas, particularly those requiring venture capital, may be better financed by other institutions. The banks may well be able to help in this area, because they know the people who provide such facilities. Once the venture is off the ground, the banks will be able to provide all the back-up services mentioned in this chapter.

10.2 How the banks are preparing themselves

10.2.1 Awareness

In the same way that businesses are having to prepare for the Single European Market, banks are having to do the same thing. The principles they are using are therefore of equal application to large and medium companies and firms. The managers and proprietors of small businesses have the greater problem of making themselves aware of what is going on – usually they have to do this in whatever spare time they can find. Like the banks, however, they cannot ignore it, because the competitor may take their own market away. Complacency is bad for business.

10.2.2 The opportunites for their customers

The big companies are already doing business in Europe, but Barclays believes that there is going to be a lot of potential for smaller enterprises. As one example of this, public bodies are not allowed to discriminate against businesses from other EEC Member States. Trade is also easier because of the Directives relating to the liberalisation of capital movements. Other examples are mentioned at the beginning of this book.

The banks are also conscious of the effect on individuals, which will lead to a greater movement of peoples throughout the Community. There will, for example, be a greater recognition of diplomas. Students may well do some of their courses abroad. This will all result in a greater demand for flexible financial services such as mortgages and insurances as well as personal banking. Indeed, a company sending any of its staff to work abroad will have to consider these aspects, and personnel departments as well as the accountants will have to talk to the bank managers of their respective enterprises.

10.2.3 Organisation

The banks are preparing for 1992 in the same way that they recommend to their customers, in that they too are having 1992 Company Audits (as in the booklet published by the European Commission and also distributed by Barclays Bank plc, *Europe 1992 – Developing an Active Company Approach to the European Market*). This is part of establishing a business strategy as detailed in chapter 2.

As a result of such activities, there have been some organisational changes. Its nineteen International Service Branches throughout the UK have received training and detailed materials on 1992, and the bank has appointed a European Director responsible for corporate services in the Community.

There are also overseas branches, but no-one is likely to be a pan-European banker in the foreseeable future. British banks are unlikely to make much impact in Germany, which already has a strong national banking system. The high street branches of Barclays in France and Spain are, for example, just like their counterparts in those countries. Different local laws and tastes affect banking as other aspects of business.

Barclays, like other banks, is therefore tackling these issues in various ways, so that they can offer a service to the UK company expanding its activities into other European countries. In order to fill the gaps it has correspondent banks throughout Europe. Many of the other aspects are mentioned later in this chapter.

10.2.4 Staff training

Because no-one can be expected to know everything, high street bank managers cannot be expected to have all the detail of EEC trade at their fingertips. They must, however, have sufficient background, and know enough to guide customers to the right services offered by the bank. Department of Trade and Industry courses are being organised for them. Relevant staff are attending in-house courses and seminars or will be undergoing distance learning courses with the aid of modern technology.

Barclays is also concerned to ensure that its customers are made aware of the potential of the Single European Market. Several local seminars have already been organised.

10.2.5 Lessons for businesspeople

All the major UK banks will be taking similar steps to those noted above, and businesses should be doing the same. They should in particular be thinking of the effects of possible extra competition from overseas or of the potential increased business for themselves. This is part of the 1992 Audit mentioned in *10.2.3* above. At the same time staff, in particular those involved in marketing and sales, must learn about the Single European Market.

10.3   Market research – how the banks can help

Although each business should do its own market research into the possibility of new markets for its products and services, the banks can provide some limited help. This can either be in the form of general publications or of more specific information about potential customers.

Barclays, like other banks, obviously has its own specialist analysts, who prepare papers on economic trends for internal guidance. Their main purpose is to help the bank manage risks, but no doubt some of such information could be made available on request. Papers on specific industries such as foodstuffs, chemicals, etc. are produced from time to time, but are aimed at the investment market. All this, anyway, is of a general nature, and similar detail can be obtained from other sources such as the Statistical Office of the European Communities.

The banks in addition issue various bulletins such as country reports, and these are directed at customers. There are also various product guides giving general information about exporting, letters of credit, trade aid and financial services in general.

10.4 | Trade Development Service

A useful service offered by Barclays in the context of business expansion is its Trade Development Service. For a small fee (currently £100 per country) the bank will help a business looking for new export customers or new sources of supply.

A form has to be completed, and obviously full details of the products or services required or on offer have to be given. In the latter case at least ten brochures should be provided. Although the bank does not require them to be in any language other than English, serious exporters should have their product literature translated and printed professionally. A glossy publication on to which has been attached a typed translation in general will not do. These days many brochures contain product information in several languages, while other companies produce one for each language.

In addition to this the enquirer can specify the size of orders being sought or those organisations not to be contacted. Such detail will help to ensure that the right response is obtained.

Once the formalities have been completed the bank then starts to do the research in various ways. Overseas' branches or correspondent banks will be contacted. International trade directories and computer data bases will be useful sources of information.

At the end of all this the enquirer will receive details of three firm contacts within six months. If the bank should fail in this objective, then half the fee will be returned, and Barclays reports that it rarely has to do this.

It is therefore a useful service for businesses without access to sophisticated sources of information, yet whose products have an export potential.

10.5	**The business plan**

10.5.1 General principles

A company seeking to set up a subsidiary in another European country (or anywhere else for that matter) usually cannot afford to do so out of its own resources. Such expansion has to be financed, and the bank is generally requested to put up the money. It will not do so unless it is convinced that the scheme has some chance of success. This convincing is done by means of a business plan produced as a result of the strategy detailed in chapter 2.

Such work must be done by the professionals, usually the accountants and marketing people, and smaller companies will often have to obtain outside help. This outside help would normally be their auditors, who may work with a firm of management consultants. The latter would often be needed to do the detailed market research needed to back up the accounting forecasts. Many firms of accountants will also need help in writing the report to make it interesting to read – they may do excellent work in producing the figures, but they may not necessarily have the writing skills.

Although the director responsible for the business plan may have delegated the job to others, he or she must ensure that it is done correctly. The final report may contain a mass of statistics and forecasts, and all these will be needed by the bank. On their own they will not impress the bank manager, because at the first glance he or she will be looking for the following information:

(1) a simple description of what is intended, why, and the benefits both to the company and the bank by their respective participation,

(2) a description of what is needed from the bank as well as of the other finance that the company is

investing from its own resources or those of its shareholders,

(3) a summary cash flow forecast backing up the description,

(4) summary profit & loss and balance sheet forecasts.

All this should be on as few pages as possible. (1) and (2) for example should ideally be on not more than two or three pages, and in any event summarised on the first paragraph or two on the first page. As mentioned in 11.4, 'keep it simple, stupid!' at this stage. (3) and (4) may then take up a page each.

Parts (1) and (2) are, however, the most important parts of the plan, because their objective is to sell the idea to the bank. The style of writing in the rest of the document may be a more restrained description of markets and plans, but that section must be more lively as in copywriting or selling. If it fails to get across the enthusiasm and the benefits of the plan, then the bank is less likely to be interested.

Because this section of the plan is intended to sell the idea, sales techniques must be used. A bank manager will be pleased to see that the result will be a percentage increase in profits, but will be more interested to be told that a more profitable company will bring more business to his or her bank.

This section must then be followed by the detailed back-up, and a format is suggested in *10.5.2* below. If this is likely to be complicated, e.g. a prospective purchase of a business with fifty stores, a forecast for each one, and details of those to be sold, then the resultant bulky document may be better presented separately from the summary mentioned above.

The plan should be as attractively presented as possible, because this is part of selling the idea to the providers of finance. In this day and age such a goal is easier to achieve by means of a combination of computer equipment and programs. Some programs can incorporate graphs and diagrams, which all help to make the presentation more attractive. It may be possible to include colour photographs or brochures of the product. The plan should then be placed in an attractive binder. Modern printing techniques as just mentioned should achieve all this cheaply, and the results using these techniques are an indication of the professionalism and competence of the prospective borrower.

10.5.2 Contents of a business plan

Each business plan should be tailored to fit the circumstances of what is intended. A suggested format is as follows:

(1) list of contents,

(2) a simple description of what is intended, why and the benefits both to the company and the bank by their respective participation,

(3) a description of what is needed from the bank as well as of the other finance that the company is investing from its own resources or those of its shareholders,

(4) a summary cash flow forecast backing up the description,

(5) summary profit & loss and balance sheet forecasts,

(6) a detailed description of the plan,

(7) basis (e.g. economic statistics, market research results) on which the plan has been compiled,

(8) details (e.g. time scales, number of employees required, etc.) of how the plan is to be implemented,

(9) structure of the new business (e.g. organisation chart),

(10) histories of the directors and senior managers,

(11) detailed cash flow forecast,

(12) detailed profit and loss forecast,

(13) detailed balance sheet forecast,

(14) detailed source and application of funds forecast,

(15) bases on which the forecasts have been prepared,

(16) sensitivity analysis,

(17) relevant accounting ratios (gearing, etc.),

(18) previous accounts (if the plan is expansion by means of acquisition of an exisiting business, then the accounts of that enterprise should also be included.

Amplification of some of these points is contained in the following sections.

10.5.3 Finance from own resources

Where interest rates are high, large amounts of borrowed money can be a drain on a business's resources. This is just one of the reasons why a bank will want to know if the proprietors or shareholders are going to put their own money into the expansion plans.

That aspect is amplified in the section on accounting ratios in *10.5.11* below, but there is another important reason. The bank is being asked to take a risk, so will want to know if the people who own the business are confident enough to back it with their cash.

Borrowing of course usually has to be secured, and businesspeople may be frustrated by what they see as a conservative attitude of the banks. Larger companies will be able to offer the business itself as security in the form of a debenture.

Smaller businesses will do this as well, but often the directors or proprietors will have to give personal guarantees. This means that the family home is at risk if things go wrong. This is another reason why banks sometimes appear to be cautious lenders – they do not like to turn people out of house and home.

10.5.4 Market research

The bank must of course be convinced that there is a good reason for the expansion plan. They can be persuaded by the following:

(1) a firm supply contract for the output of the expanded business,

(2) expansion by means of the purchase of another viable business,

(3) existing resources (e.g. production capacity) are insufficient to meet demand,

(4) good market research.

Although not necessary in every case, numbers (1) to (3) should ideally be backed up by (4). If the intention is to expand overseas because it is believed that there is a market for the product, then market research is essential.

Small companies in these circumstances may well find the appointment of a market research firm very expensive. They will then have to do their own in-house exercise, but do it they must. A bank will not lend money purely on the hope of a larger market overseas.

Some help in this respect may be obtained from the figures published by the Commission and by other organisations, such as Chambers of Commerce, and which are mentioned elsewhere in this book, in particular in chapter 3. Background statistics about specific industries can be obtained from the various publications mentioned in Appendix 2, certain computer data bases, and trade associations.

10.5.5 How the plan is to be achieved

No money will be lent if there is any doubt about the capabilities of the company to achieve the expansion. An important part of the presentation to the bank or financial institution is a section on how the plan is to be achieved. This may be in the form of a timetable, and if this is very complicated, a diagram in the form of a critical path analysis could be added. For people who know such a technique, there are computer programs which will help in the preparation of the diagram.

All this preparation work will serve another purpose, in that it will provide targets for the company to achieve. This will be an important working document, although things will not always go to plan. Even in those circumstances the work will not be wasted. Plans can always be amended, and if it is a detailed one in the form of a critical path analysis produced by a computer program, it is easy to see what effect any delay will have on the rest of the timetable. There can be an ordered exit from the situation.

10.5.6 Structure of the business

The bank or financial institution will also want to know how the expansion fits in with the existing business. If the plan is merely to increase UK production facilities to satisfy an anticipated overseas demand, there is not likely to be any change. A new factory in another country or a purchase of an existing business overseas leads to different considerations.

One of these is whether or not this aspect of the business is to result in a new company incorporated in a different country. There may have to be a new UK holding company. These all have legal and financial effects, but the professional team, such as that mentioned in 11.2, will give advice. That will have to be pointed out in the presentation to the bank or financial institution.

Even if the expansion involves no change to the existing companies, numbers of employees are likely to increase. An organisational chart should be included with the plan, so both the company and the bank or financial institution can be satisfied that staff will be controlled, and that the directors or managers do not have too many people reporting to them.

An organisational chart like this will also help the bank decide if it requires what is known as 'key man insurance'. A business may rely heavily on the skills of one person, and it would be a disaster for the business if that person should be incapacitated due to illness or injury or if he or she should die. The bank or financial institution will then insist on this insurance, which will pay out in such circumstances. This will protect not only the bank's invest-ment, but also the interests of shareholders and other creditors in that there will be cash if the company should cease trading. This insurance may be required for several of the business's senior executives.

10.5.7 Histories of the directors and senior managers

If the bank manager knows the people well, infor-mation about the working histories and qualifications of the directors and senior managers may at first sight seem to be irrelevant. The bank manager will not, however, be the final decision-maker as to whether or not the finance is to be provided. If the requirements are high, then other people such as financial analysts will have to give their opinions. The ultimate decision may have to be taken at a higher level.

It is therefore important to show that the people with important jobs to do in the business are capable of handling the new situation. If the finance is needed to purchase a new business, the bank will want to know about the senior people who are being taken over with it.

10.5.8 Controls

Any business plan should mention how the expand-ed operation will be controlled. This will usually include the following:

(1) monitoring of sales,
(2) financial budgets,
(3) internal audit,
(4) trouble shooting,
(5) reports to management,
(6) management meetings,
(7) communication of objectives from the directors and management.

A small business which is to open, say, just one factory or warehouse across the Channel will not need anything sophisticated, but it will still need all the elements mentioned above in some form or other.

10.5.9 Points to be considered for the financial forecasts

Although the principles in compiling a financial forecast are the same for any country, there will be some different factors – usually taxation! Subject to the nature of the business a check list should include the following points:

(1) capital costs of the expansion (e.g. shopfitting, purchase of the new company, purchase of the lease, etc.),

(2) legal costs (including conveyancing and taxes if relevant),

(3) consultant's fees,

(4) accountants' fees,

(5) set-up costs (including executives' travel and purchase of opening stock),

(6) removal expenses for executives,

(7) rent and rates or local property taxes,

(8) insurance,

(9) interest on the extra borrowing,

(10) bank charges,

(11) light and heat,

(12) wages and salaries plus any local payroll tax,

(13) audit fees,

(14) loan repayments,

(15) travel,

(16) post, packing and stationery (note that new stationery may be required and it may be appropriate to include that expense under set-up costs),

(17) purchases,

(18) sales and seasonal variations,

(19) provision for bad debts,

(20) depreciation,

(21) VAT (each country at the moment has different rates),

(22) taxation in general,

(23) extra cash provided by the directors, proprietors or shareholders,

(24) contingencies,

(25) carriage,

(26) discounts allowed or received,

(27) commissions payable or receivable,

(28) general expenses (including petty cash),

(29) leasing or hire purchase (note that in Greece and Portugal what is called leasing may amount to hire purchase).

10.5.10 Bases of the figures

Any lender will want to be assured that the figures have been prepared on a logical basis, and the purpose of the notes to the forecast will be to explain what this is. It will contain many factors which will depend on the nature of the business, e.g.:

(1) number of anticipated customers and amount of sales per customer,

(2) number of units of output from the factory (with perhaps some forecast cost accounts analysis),

(3) basis of the calculation of stock holdings (e.g. number of days' sales),

(4) basis of the calculation of trade debtors or trade creditors (e.g. number of days of sales or purchases (both including VAT) respectively),

(5) an analysis of expense creditors outstanding at any time,

(6) the basis on which the purchases have been calculated (e.g. a percentage of sales),

(7) the interest rates used in the calculation of loan repayments,

(8) an analysis of the capital and set-up costs,

(9) the basis of depreciation and any provisions such as bad debts,

(10) any other relevant bases (e.g. a reduced or

increased cost of freight because of the opening of a new branch abroad).

The figures must be prepared in a logical way. The cash flow forecast will in most trading, for example, include VAT in receipts, but the sales figure in the profit and loss account will be net. The difference between the two will be accounted for by payments of the tax recorded in the cash flow and by the VAT creditor in the forecast closing balance sheet.

If this is prepared by means of a computer and a spreadsheet, it should be possible to achieve this by means of formulae within the program. If the bank or financial institution requests a change in the figures (and they often do!) it can be done quickly.

10.5.11 Accounting ratios

In addition to the basis on which the figures are produced, the bank's analysts will test the business's past and forecast performance by checking various ratios. They will, for example, check the figure of liquid assets (cash and assets) against that of current liabilities (creditors payable within one year). The ratio of approximately 1:1 is an indication that the cash flow is about right. Some of these figures can be measured against those of companies in the same industry. A business plan for fund-raising purposes should cover a reasonable period (at least two years), so the value of these ratios is that they will show trends over that time.

One particularly important figure relates to what is known as gearing. This is a measure of the company's borrowing, and although in certain circumstances there are advantages in a high gearing, banks as a whole do not like a business to have too high borrowings. In any event such debt would have to be well covered by assets.

It is quite helpful therefore to include these ratios in a business plan, because it may help to save the bank's time. Many enterprises do not do so – sometimes because the figures reveal weaknesses! They are quite easy to prepare in a spreadsheet on a computer. It is furthermore possible to buy, for example, an addition to a spreadsheet program *Lotus 1 2 3*, which contains the formulae within it.

The main ratios are as follows:
(1) fixed interest shares plus long-term liabilities to equity (gearing ratio),
(2) equity to total capital employed,
(3) liquid assets to current liabilities (mentioned above),
(4) current assets to current liabilities,
(5) stock to working capital,
(6) fixed assets to long-term liabilities (generally a ratio of 2:1 is considered to be the least requirement),
(7) net capital employed to fixed assets,
(8) net capital employed to total liabilities,
(9) gross profit as a percentage of sales,
(10) net sales to net capital employed,
(11) net sales to equity interest (ordinary share capital plus reserves) – a low rate could indicate that the company is undertrading and not using its financial resources effectively, while a high ratio may indicate either high profits or that route to insolvency known as overtrading,
(12) net profit as a percentage of sales,
(13) cost of sales divided by average stock at cost (stock turnover),
(14) debtors divided by average daily credit sales including VAT (number of days taken to collect debts),
(15) as (14) but for creditors and purchases on credit,
(16) earnings per share,
(17) price/earnings ratio (price per share divided by earnings per share).

Some of these figures will be mentioned in the business plan to show the basis on which the figures are prepared, e.g. (14), but as already mentioned historical figures will also have to be produced.

There are other figures which affect specific industries. A project for a new restaurant should, for example, include information about sales per cover.

10.5.12 Format of the forecasts

Although there are many ways of showing the figures, the best way is to keep it simple and use the generally accepted accounting formats. This is a must at the summary stage, although the back-up paperwork may be very complicated if the expansion is likely to be complicated. It must, however, be possible to follow the figures through the various documents (i.e. there must be what the accountants call an audit trail).

10.5.13 Sensitivity analysis

Banks and financial institutions will often ask 'What is the downside?' or 'Is there a sensitivity analysis?' What they want to know is whether or not anyone has looked at what happens if targets are not met. More rarely they will want to know what happens if results are better than expected.

The plan should therefore include appropriate alternatives and perhaps a break-even point.

10.5.14 Alternative sources of finance

An expansion plan may be turned down by a bank, although it is well thought out and logical. The reason for this often arises out of the funding proposal – the company wants to borrow too much money. The bank would prefer cash to be provided out of an issue of shares.

All is not lost, because the would-be borrower should ask how the bank would help. All high street banks have contacts with venture capital financiers, and may be willing to lend at least part of the finance provided that the remainder comes from such a different source.

In that case the business requiring the finance will have to do some rethinking. Some financiers may be willing to provide money in exchange for shares, but will insist on the opportunity to sell out in three to five years if all has gone well. Although they may be happy for the company to be managed in the same way, they may want the right to appoint one or more directors. The existing managers and directors must be prepared for this much closer relationship with the provider of finance.

In any event, if an approach is made to a prospective financier other than a bank, a business plan produced in accordance with the principles mentioned in the previous paragraphs will still be needed.

10.5.15 Grants

Banks can advise on any grants that may be available such as those provided by the EEC to certain deprived areas. One of these can pay for the cost of consultancy to businesses in those regions.

10.6 Banking overseas

As has already been mentioned there is no pan-European bank in the sense of being able to offer high street type banking services in all of the countries. Barclays, for example, has operations in eleven out of twelve Community countries, and whilst it is particularly well represented in Spain and France, it has few branches in West Germany and none in Scandinavia. The other UK banks are similarly strong in some countries but weak in others. This gap can be covered by 'correspondent bankers', which means that where a UK bank does not have a strong presence, it can make the necessary introductions to an overseas branch, who will probably have reciprocal arrangements for introducing its customers to a UK branch.

10.7 Exporting – reducing risks

It is possible to obtain Export Credit Guarantee Department (ECGD) Insurance for certain export contracts.

All the major banks provide various schemes linked into the government ECGD schemes. Barclays Bank also operates a Smaller Exports Scheme where, subject to certain conditions, it will lend money against presentation of the export documents. This scheme can be covered by the bank's own ECGD insurance.

Selling into the Single European Market, however, will eventually be regarded as merely an extension of the home market.

10.8 | Other ways to increase business

The European Community has a programme of funding projects in those countries in Africa, the Caribbean and Pacific linked to the EEC by the Lomé Convention as well as others in the Mediterranean and Asia. For UK enterprises this can provide business opportunities either in the supply of goods or services or both. Consultants with the right skills can also benefit from the programme.

Barclays Bank, for example, therefore:
(1) provides up to two years advance information on projects, and sometimes supplies tender documents,
(2) issues bank guarantees with the aim of reducing to a minimum the periods during which they are marked against the customer's liability to the bank,
(3) provides non-recourse financing of up to 100% of the contract price at favourable rates to cover the two- to four-month period between the signing of the provisional acceptance of the tender and the receipt of the payment for the goods.

A typical procedure is as follows:
(1) the bank gives advance information on projects,
(2) the bank's customer (the supplier) acts on the information and submits a tender to the country in which the project is being undertaken,
(3) if the tender is accepted, and the supplier agrees to go ahead the European Commission (EC), who is to foot the bill, is informed,

(4) the supplier also contacts the EC to request that the down payment be made to the bank,

(5) once that payment has been received the bank notifies the supplier who can then ship the goods,

(6) the recipient sends a provisional acceptance to the EC, which informs the supplier,

(7) that supplier informs the bank, which provides the non-recourse finance.

Consultants should note that:

(1) they have to be registered with the Directorate General for Development,

(2) local EC representatives can award contracts for up to 40,000 ECUs without consultation with Brussels,

(3) above that amount there is a system of short lists,

(4) procedures can vary from case to case.

Despite the paperwork needed to become registered, this is an opportunity for consultants to increase their business with the aid of EEC money and to help less privileged countries to develop their potential.

10.9 | Credit control and overseas creditors

10.9.1 Letters of credit

Letters of credit should become much rarer in a Single European Market because of their complication and cost. It is a written undertaking given by a bank on behalf of an importer to pay the exporter an amount of money within a specified time provided the exporter presents documents which conform with the terms laid down in the letter of credit. For countries in the EEC the system is more appropriate for large one-off consignments of goods, and is not recommended for frequent transactions. The system is as follows:

(1) In theory both buyer and seller agree terms of the credit, but in practice the buyer imposes them.

(2) The buyer then requests his or her bank to open

the letter of credit, and it requests a bank in the seller's country to advise the credit.

(3) When the goods have been dispatched, the seller then presents the documents at the advising bank

(4) If the documents, such as invoices, bills of lading or airway bills, certificates of insurance, comply with what is demanded by the letter of credit, then the advising bank will pay, negotiate or accept the bill of exchange accompanying the documents in accordance with the terms of that credit. It sends the documents to the issuing bank and obtains payment.

There are various forms of letter of credit either revocable or irrevocable. A revocable credit is one which can be cancelled or amended without the seller's knowledge – definitely to be avoided. The most common is irrevocable and unconfirmed. The most desirable is irrevocable and confirmed in that the advising bank undertakes to pay in accordance with the letter of credit provided that all the documents are in order. The seller, however, has to pay an extra charge.

Most banks can help with advice and the presentation of documents for their customers, and their advice can be very helpful. The practice of Barclays (like some others) to establish business centres means that the exporter can consult the experts. This is essential for exports to some countries which demand very precise documentation and whose governments change the regulations from time to time.

That of course is not a problem in the EEC, and the trend is for open credit or payment against invoice transactions as noted below.

10.9.2 Open credit or payment against invoice

Many businesses treat customers in other countries of the Common Market in the same way as domestic purchasers. This means that they will be offered the same credit terms such as 'thirty days from date of invoice' or 'payment against invoice'.

The credit control procedures should be the same, and this will include the normal bank reference or status report (not forgetting the usual supplier's reference). This is obtained in the normal way through an application to the seller's branch, and it is important to specify the amount of credit to be granted. References are often blandly worded, so it is important to read them carefully to find their true meaning. For example, an unqualified ' . . . would not enter into any transactions they were unable to fulfil . . . ' should put the seller on his or her guard.

10.9.3 Factoring

Banks usually have international factoring companies, which means that the seller can obtain cash on the strength of the invoices issued. The factoring company then has the task of obtaining the money, and although this service is achieved for a mixture of a fee and interest until payment is received, there are two advantages to outweigh these considerations:

(1) the seller receives cash immediately,

(2) the seller's credit control department does not have to try and obtain payment from someone who does not speak English.

10.9.4 Forfaiting

Forfaiting is more suitable for bigger one-off deals, because the forfaiting bank takes over the exporter's receivables for a discount on a non-recourse basis. The bank must of course be brought into the picture at an early stage in the negotiations, because it will require a guarantee usually from the buyer's bank. This enables the seller to offer credit terms on the transaction.

10.9.5 Quoting the customer

Forfaiting and factoring both involve extra costs, and should be be incorporated in the calculation of the price to the customer.

Other factors are the cost of freight, so a company which quotes an all-inclusive price for delivery in the UK may have to think again when it comes to exports across the frontier. The following expressions are often used in quotations:

> *ex works* or *ex warehouse* – the buyer has to pay for transport from the seller's premises
>
> *fob* or *free on board* – freight charges will be paid up to the time the goods are swung across the ship's rail
>
> *c&f* or *cost and freight* – the seller will pay the freight charges for delivery but not the insurance
>
> *cif* or *cost insurance freight* – as c&f but the seller will also pay the insurance.

10.10 Foreign currency accounts

Businesses which buy and sell goods in specific foreign currencies should consider opening bank accounts in those currencies through their own UK bank. This saves costs, in that charges for changing money in relation to each transaction into sterling do not have to be made. If the account is to be in credit, then a deposit account can be opened.

10.11 More sophisticated foreign currency control

10.11.1 Exchange risk

One of the problems of buying and selling in foreign currencies is that exchange rates fluctuate, yet overseas buyers wish to be invoiced in their own currencies. The UK has not joined the exchange rate mechanism of the European Monetary System, so sterling is more susceptible to variations against other European currencies. This problem for the seller can in part be solved by the foreign exchange forward market. The procedure in outline is:

> (1) the seller knows that a foreign buyer is to pay for the goods in a foreign currency at a stipulated time in the future, say in ninety days,

(2) he or she therefore enters into an agreement to buy sterling for that foreign currency at a rate of exchange fixed at the outset. Banks can obviously help in this respect and others such as foreign currency options, where there is a right but no obligation to buy or sell the currency.

10.11.2 European Currency Units

Although there are no coins or notes in European Currency Units (ECUs) businesses can use them. At this time it is only appropriate for larger companies, some of which do their internal inter-branch accounting in this currency. Enterprises doing a lot of business in Europe could well consider invoicing some of their customers in ECUs. It can save time in administration of various currencies, and is easier to control in terms of exchange rate fluctuations. Any such procedure will have to be after consultation with the bank.

10.12 | Travelling

Other services for frequent overseas travel include:
(1) supplies of travellers' cheques or currency,
(2) cheque guarantee cards such as Barclaycard,
(3) expatriate services such as pensions and invest-ment services.

10.13 | Summary

Banks therefore are an important part of any plans by a business to take advantage of the Single European Market. The following areas are particularly important:
(1) the provision of sales leads or information about prospective EEC-funded contracts,
(2) the provision of information about sources of EEC funds,
(3) the providers of finance (or information about alternative sources of finance), but the prospective borrower must prepare a detailed business plan,

(4) the provision of credit control services,

(5) the provision of advice and help in relation to overseas banking.

PART 3
A case study – retailing

CHAPTER 11
A case study – retailing

11.1 Introduction

Most of this chapter has been compiled from information provided by the Sock Shop International plc, although the author has added his own impressions and opinions. Many of the lessons drawn from this experience are appropriate for manufacturers and other businesses, not just for retailers.

11.2 The team

11.2.1 Head of the team

Many businesses are appointing a person who is responsible for European affairs, and the Sock Shop has given a director this responsibility. It emphasises the importance being given by companies to the advent of the Single European Market, but the business objectives and the skills of the enterprise must be analysed.

Other businesses may decide that their objectives are to increase their market share from the UK, in which case it may be appropriate to appoint a marketing director to do the job. ICL has set up a European Strategy Board, while international companies such as the Eastman Kodak Company already has a Vice President with responsibilities for the European Region. In this respect multi-nationals already have the structure to deal with any changes introduced by the Single European Market.

Small businesses cannot, however, ignore what is happening, because everyone throughout the EEC is being encouraged to consider expansion beyond their national boundaries. This could result in extra competition at home or abroad, so at the very least someone in the enterprise must be given the responsibility of keeping an eye on what is happening.

11.2.2 The composition of the team

Once a decision has been made to expand the business into another European country, it is essential to build up a strong team of professionals including:

Property people
Lawyers
Accountants
Bankers
Insurance brokers.

11.3 | The check list

An important assignment for the person responsible for a plan to expand into another country is the establishment of a check list of things to do. According to the Sock Shop International plc, this continuously changes as experience is built up. That view seems to be supported by the DTI, which has already changed the check list included with the 1992 information packs.

Check lists are mentioned in more detail in other parts of this book, but the Sock Shop International plc particularly mentioned the following:

(1) is it cheaper to ship the goods from the UK or to use local manufacturers?

(2) what are you allowed to do in relation to the refurbishment of the building?

(3) timing,

(4) how far can local people be used in setting up the new enterprise?

(5) are there any potential problems relating to Trade Unions?

(6) are there any differences in relation to merchandising?

(7) what is the competition?

(8) a system for accounting records,

(9) are any government or other grants available?

11.4 | The business plan

Most businesses cannot afford to expand with the aid of their own cash resources, so they have to borrow money from banks or other financial institutions, who must be given a business plan. This must sell the idea effectively, so it is important to observe the general 'KISS' rule – 'keep it simple, stupid!'. The bank or financial institution must be able to see quickly what is intended. Because some businesses have a close working relationship with their banks, they may not need to produce an aggressive selling document. It is at times like these that there is a real benefit of keeping their bank managers regularly informed of what is going on.

According to the Sock Shop International plc the main ingredients of its business plan were:

Finance-raising plan

Selling plan

Working plan.

It therefore concentrated on the requirements of the business for its expansion, and did not have to sell the basic concept to the bank. Other enterprises, which are looking for finance from other sources, or which do not have such a close relationship with their banks, will have to spend some time on this aspect of the plan.

11.5 | The people

An important element of success for any business is to ensure that the right people are appointed. According to the Sock Shop International plc the management of the US operation was 'a unique combination of input from England joined with people from US retailing'.

In addition to a pioneering team mentioned in 11.6 below, trouble-shooters from the UK will be needed as part of the essential monitoring procedures. Otherwise a programme of local recruitment will have to be established together with the essential staff training.

11.6 | Marketing and research

Although the Sock Shop International plc obviously subscribes to the maxim that 'selling is matching needs', it also realises that the process can be reversed in order to create the need. Cultural differences are also recognised in that, for example, the operation in the USA started with less than 20% own-label brands in the shops. Six months later that had increased to 50%.

The operation has to be integrated with the existing operation. Decisions have to be made about local retailing, local buying and local property, and how they can be mixed with what the company is doing.

It is, however, necessary firstly to research areas where new business can be obtained, and the Sock Shop International plc achieves this by sending its own personnel to visit new territory. The company generally is good at doing things for itself, because it takes too much time to delegate some of the research as noted in 11.8 below.

Such research can take the form of a pioneering team of UK employees, who look round a prospective area. Local bookstalls are often a good source of information, as they may contain business publications covering such things as employment. Chambers of Commerce can also be helpful.

The staff of the Sock Shop International plc obviously have the skills to do this research, but this may not suit all businesses. Some details as to the sources of information will be found in Appendix 1, but the list of professionals mentioned in *11.2.2* above may have to include market researchers.

11.7 | Property

Site location for any business is also an important ingredient of its success. Retailers are obviously concerned about the potential passing trade. The Sock Shop International plc, for example, trades from sites at railway or underground stations, so is concerned to survey the passenger flows. It has to find out how the prospective site matches the need of the commuters. Manufacturers or distributors, on the other hand, are more worried about communications and the availability of suitably qualified people.

The Sock Shop International plc has a particularly good approach once the prospective sites have been identified. Most businesses merely negotiate the lease with the landlord on the basis of the terms on offer.

Such negotiation is an extension of a principal of selling, i.e. that of matching needs. The prospective landlord is therefore interviewed about his or her needs.

Most landlords, for example, are interested in rent, so one attraction may be a rental based on turnover. Once they learn of the turnover per square foot achieved by the Sock Shop International plc, they become very interested in what may be on offer. Other landlords may, however, also be concerned about the environment, so the prospective tenant will talk about the quality of the means by which the business is to be presented.

11.8 | Government departments

Some businesses may find approaches to government departments for market research too time-consuming, but that will not be true in every case. Exporters or potential exporters, for example, should be able to obtain useful information from the Department of Trade.

Government departments can, however, be useful sources of money in the form of grants to encourage trade in less favoured regions. The Sock Shop International plc has found that accountants or lawyers are the most useful sources of information as to how or where these can be obtained.

11.9   Trading names and trade marks

For the Sock Shop International plc the protection of company and trading names, logos and the like is an important area. The lawyers will have a lot of work to do, and a hard line must be taken at the first sign of any infringement. Any business with a good idea and an associated trading name or logo must look ahead, and prevent such problems.

In addition to the problems of this sort a business has to ensure that it too complies with the local laws relating to trading standards. Labels have to contain details about sizes, washing instructions and textile content in accordance with local laws. The professional team mentioned in 11.2 will have to include people who can advise on the correct procedures. The Sock Shop International plc commented on the 'fantastic help' given by the lawyers.

11.10   Shipping

The Sock Shop International plc obviously has a shipping department, whose manager spends a lot of time on research. It is essential to appoint good shipping agents, as the company does not want any unpleasant surprises. Despite the simplification of the paperwork the forms still require a lot of detail. These must be completed correctly.

Distances obviously affect distribution systems, and the logistics of business in Europe are covered in chapter 6.

The weather is another factor, and the Sock Shop International plc provides its New York warehouse with snow removal equipment. Such measures are not needed in Paris, because it is part of a complex providing these services. This point illustrates the detail needed in planning a successful overseas expansion scheme.

11.11 | Collaboration

There are some limited possibilities in this respect of collaboration. A group of tenants, for example, may get together if the landlord is not publicising a shopping centre sufficiently or as promised. Again, if a larger site than is needed is on offer, a deal by two or more businesses can secure the property.

11.12 | Languages

Languages have never been a problem for the Sock Shop International plc, because they have always found staff with the required languages among their own employees. It is important, however, that at least some of the overseas staff speak English.

Some companies have a common administrative language. One Dutch multi-national uses English, but there can still be problems of communication. That company, for example, insists on calling differences between actual accounting figures and those in the budget are known as 'mutations', but English accountants call them 'variances'. These literal translations from various languages can cause much misunderstanding.

11.13 | Different rules and regulations

There may be a Single European Market, but as explained in other parts of the book many differences still remain. These will not be a great problem for those companies which have built up a good team of professional advisers (as noted in 11.2 above). National regulations concerning product safety and the like are generally not applicable to a retail organisation selling low-tech goods.

Despite this the occasional problem can still arise. The French equivalent of the UK Trading Standards Officer will demand that prices should be displayed in the window, although this is not a requirement in the UK.

| 11.14 | **Administration** |

11.14.1 Accounts

The Sock Shop International plc appoints a local bookkeeper, who will obviously have the required knowledge of the local rules relating to the operation of a payroll, VAT and bank accounts. The subsidiary's financial accounts are initially processed by the UK computer system. The overseas staff therefore complete documentation, and send it here. This system obviously has to change as noted in *11.14.2* below when the business expands.

Accounts departments are not just information gatherers and should play an active role in the control of the business. The figures to update cash flow forecasts and budgets all help in management decision making.

Such attention to detail is obviously an important factor in building up good relationships with the banks and financial institutions supplying the money for expansion.

11.14.2 Computers

With expansion it is necessary to install more sophisticated systems. The branches of the Sock Shop International plc are about to be networked into the one computer. An EPOS (Electronic Point of Sale) is being developed to serve the stores and provide an even more efficient stock replenishment system. More information about computer systems to assist in European expansion is to be found in chapter 9.

11.14.3 Sales information

In this day and age businesses only succeed if their executives are given up-to-date information, so that they can react to rapidly changing situations. Computers can be an important part of this strategy.

Sales figures for the UK and France relating to the Sock Shop International plc for the previous day are available every day by 9.00 a.m. For comparison purposes sales figure for the same period in the previous year.

Gone are the days when slow computer systems could not provide the information for several days, and only outline figures were available from branches. Businesses have to set up systems to provide information quickly.

11.14.4 Insurance

In the experience of the Sock Shop International plc there has been little difference between UK insurance and that of other countries. Only the US market has proved difficult because of the general nervousness of product liability claims. This could change, because some countries have adopted strict liability in relation to products sold to consumers as noted in 5.4.

11.14.5 Travel

Although the local people may be good, executives from head office still must go and have a look at what is going on. Long distances mean that much more effort has to be put into maintaining high standards. Travel also involves a lot of wasted time. An executive can visit many stores in a capital city in one day, whereas it takes all day to go to one outlet in a provincial town; this cannot be ignored. This travel time can be used more efficiently by use of mobile telephones, fax machines and computers.

11.15 Successful strategy

The experience of those already with overseas branches or subsidiaries shows that the ingredients for a successful business expansion abroad are:

(1) careful research,

(2) the appointment of a good team of professionals,

(3) a well-prepared business plan,

(4) the establishment of a good relationship with the providers of finance,

(5) good administration,

(6) the selection of the right staff in the overseas subsidiary,

(7) sound liaison between the staff in the UK and

those in the overseas subsidiary,

(8) proper monitoring of results,

(9) a practical approach,

(10) no compromise on high standards.

Whatever a company does, there are bound to be some limiting factors in terms of people, finance or administration. To get it all right executives involved in the expansion will have to put in some long hours of hard work.

PART 4
Appendices

APPENDIX 1
Statistics – a brief survey of the Common Market

1	**Basic economics**

Without the Common Market a business in the UK wishing to export to Europe would be faced with eleven different countries, lots of complicated paperwork, differing laws affecting international trade, and all sorts of other problem affecting technical standards, health and safety, industrial relations and the like. The Single European Act should result in a market of 322 million people, more than the inhabitants of either the USA or the USSR.

Differences will of course remain. People do not have the same tastes or speak the same language even within one country. There will still be some technical differences – the UK square pin electrical plug will remain as an oddity in relation to the round pin ones in the other countries, where there are also similar problems as between themselves.

Each business is different, so will have to do its own research. This will be essential if the expansion is to be financed by means of bank borrowing because, as pointed out in chapter 10, the potential lender will need the information for two reasons. It will help it to evaluate the proposal, and will also be evidence that the potential borrower has researched the matter thoroughly.

Economics will also help a company in making decisions about its strategic plan in relation to the Single Market. The very fact of a potential market of 322 million people, where trade is encouraged between Member States, is an important benefit to a business in the UK seeking to expand its activities.

2 | Centres of population

2.1 General

One consideration for a business that is expanding beyond its own national frontier is the size of the market, because this will be one factor in deciding where to concentrate its activities. Some help will be found in statistics such as the following:

Country	Population 1976 (thousands)	Population (latest figures) (thousands)	% increase/ (decrease)	People per square kilometre
Belgium	9,818	9,858	0.41	323
Denmark	5,073	5,114	0.81	119
France	52,983	55,170	4.13	101
Greece	9,599	9,935	3.50	75
Ireland	3,162	3,540	11.95	51
Italy	56,001	57,141	2.04	190
Luxembourg	356	367	3.09	141
The Netherlands	13,774	14,492	5.21	352
Portugal	9,448	10,157	7.50	110
Spain	35,850	38,602	7.68	76
United Kingdom	56,001	56,618	1.10	232
West Germany	61,531	61,024	(0.82)	245
Totals	313,596	322,018	2.69	143

[Sources include *Europe in Figures* (1987)]

Population as a whole is expected to grow only some 2% in the years from 1985 to 2005. A lower birth rate and an ageing population is also a factor in deciding which products to market.

2.2 Centres of population

Businesses must not only expand in the right country, but they must be based in the right area. The main regions are as follows:

Region	Population (thousands)	Region	Population (thousands)
Paris	8,710	West Yorkshire	1,480
Rhein-Ruhr	7,790	Copenhagen	1,370
London	7,680	Lisbon	1,300
Madrid	4,170	Brussels	1,280
Athens	3,030	Lyon	1,220
Milan	2,810	Glasgow	1,210
Rome	2,790	Marseille	1,110
Barcelona	2,700	Rotterdam	1,030
Naples	2,520	Lille	940
West Midlands	2,360	Amsterdam	940
Manchester	2,340	Dublin	920
West Berlin	1,870	Valencia	850
Munich	1,840	Genoa	800
Hamburg	1,620	Tyneside	780
Turin	1,480	Liverpool	750

[Source *Europe in Figures* (1987)]

The main centres of population are generally found in an axis from Manchester in the north of England to Milan in the north of Italy. The figures show the opportunities awaiting businesses wishing to take advantage of the Single European Market.

2.3 Population movements

Figures such as those mentioned in the previous two paragraphs do not always give sufficient information about regions, because people move around. We all know about the decline of certain industries such as shipbuilding in the north of England or on Clydeside. The population of the Paris region increased by 1,152,000 between 1954 and 1975 (*The Logic of Unity*, Geoffrey Parker, 1981, Longmans) while during the same period 202,907 people moved away from the Nord/Pas de Calais region.

Such figures are not the only considerations, because other factors could reverse the trends. The construction of the Channel Tunnel could, for example, make the Pas de Calais an expanding area. The EEC is also investing money in disadvantaged areas to try and encourage the establishment of new industries there.

A manufacturer in the UK may, for example, also prefer to set up a new factory in one of those areas just because of those incentives. Provided that all other factors are right, such as transport and communications, it could make good economic sense to start up in a disadvantaged region.

2.4 Disadvantaged regions

It can make good sense to start up in an area aided by the Regional Development Fund, which contributes towards the investment cost of approved industrial, tourist or service projects in the Member States. It also contributes towards the cost of infrastructure projects run by public authorities. In addition to that there is a non-quota section of the Fund, so that money can be provided for specific projects such as aid for shipbuilding areas in the UK, i.e. Strathclyde, Merseyside, Tyne and Wear.

It comprises 7.5% of the Community budget (2.3 million European Curency Units in 1985) and an indication of the countries to benefit is as follows:

Country	Share of the 1986 budget	Population as a % of the Community
Italy	21.62% to 28.79%	17.75
Spain	17.97% to 23.93%	11.99
United Kingdom	14.50% to 19.31%	17.58
Portugal	10.66% to 14.20%	3.15
Greece	8.36% to 10.64%	3.09
France	7.48% to 9.96%	17.13
Ireland	3.82% to 4.61%	1.10
West Germany	2.55% to 3.40%	18.95
Netherlands	0.68% to 0.91%	4.50
Belgium	0.61% to 0.82%	3.06
Denmark	0.34% to 0.46%	1.59
Luxembourg	0.04% to 0.06%	0.11

[Source *European Economy* (March 1988)]

These figures provide some guide to the state of each country's economy. In theory those countries whose percentage share of the EEC budget is higher than that of their population have economic problems. For most businesses it will be better to expand into areas where there is a strong economy. For others the attraction of subsidies will be more important in, for example, the setting up of a new factory. Some of those problems may, however, be the result of poor communications, and distribution of the finished product will then be difficult.

Addresses of where to obtain more information about the various grants will be found in Appendix 3.

3 | Industry

3.1 General

Large cities are not everything in that some enterprises are in the business of supplying industry. They may therefore find it better to set up new branches or outlets in those areas, where industry is concentrated. Some of the most important of these are noted in the following sections.

3.2 Triangles and other shapes

In the UK the major industrial concentrations are to be found in Central Scotland, the North and Midlands of England, South Wales and Greater London. The UK growth zone from the southeast of England to Manchester has been described as the Coffin, because of its shape.

Just over the Channel there is what is known as the Heavy Industrial Triangle of North West Europe. Its corners are the Nord coalfield of France, the Ruhr coalfield of West Germany, and the Lorraine iron-ore field.

The importance of this Triangle is emphasised by some figures. In 1984 it contained 95% of the coal production of the original six Members, and 90% of their steel production. Off-shoots from the Triangle extend into the Mid-Rhinelands, across the northern part of West Germany, and into The Netherlands.

Another industrial triangle is found between the northern Italian cities of Milan, Turin and Genoa, although there are other major industrial concentrations in Greater Paris, Lyon St Etienne and Marseilles-Fos. The main economic centre in Greece is centred on the two cities of Piraeus and Athens.

The major industrial zones are, like the centres of population, found in the area between Manchester and Milan. People have generally moved into the triangles or other industrial parts of Europe, and this is just one of the considerations that a business must take into account before making the decision to start operations in another part of Europe.

3.3 Growing and declining demand

The Directorate General for Economic and Financial Affairs has produced some figures to indicate the percentage average rate of growth or decline in domestic demand. Such statistical information is an important factor in deciding a strategy for expansion. Indeed, if such a plan is to rely on borrowed money, the bank will want to know what research into the market has been done.

	Sector Percentage change 1973–85
Office and data-processing machines	9.0
Electrical and electronic goods	3.5
Chemical and pharmaceutical products	5.3
Rubber and plastic products	2.8
Transport equipment	1.7
Food, beverages, tobacco	1.2
Paper and printing products	1.6
Industrial and agricultural machinery	−0.1
Metal products	−0.5
Miscellaneous manufactured products	−0.6
Ferrous and non-ferrous ores and metals	0.6
Textiles, leather, clothing	−0.2
Non-metallic minerals (construction materials)	−0.1

These highlight the weak demand in a recession for such commodities as coal and steel. There is, however, a high demand for computers.

3.4 Services

Business is not all manufacturing, as it includes commerce, insurance, transport, administration, catering, etc. Between 1975 and 1985 the total volume of the service sector as a percentage of the gross domestic product of the European Community increased from 47.3% to 57.2% (i.e. volume up by around 21%). It employed around 48.8% of the workforce in 1975, but by 1985 this had increased to 57.6% (i.e. volume up by 18%). This emphasises the loss of jobs from manufacturing (12% between 1980 and 1985) and agriculture (13% in the same period).

4 Transport

Another factor in the choosing of a site for business expansion is that of communications as mentioned in chapter 7. In addition to road, rail and air there is one other mode of transport which is more frequently used in many European countries than in the UK or Ireland. Half the freight of The Netherlands is carried by barges and the like on inland waterways. The percentage is smaller in West Germany, but the volume is higher. Canal transport is also important in northern France and Belgium.

5 Removal of barriers to trade

5.1 Barriers

According to the Commission there are three main barriers to the free flow of goods, services, capital and labour as follows:

(1) physical frontiers, i.e. customs controls at national borders,

(2) technical frontiers where in addition to differing regulations there is discrimination against foreign bids for the supply to public bodies,

(3) tax frontiers, e.g. differing rates of VAT.

There is no argument in principle about (1) and (2) but in the UK there is a debate as to whether or not differing rates of VAT within the Community are a hindrance to the Single European Market. It is suggested that provided there is consistency of treatment within the national boundary, inter-Community trade is not hindered.

A survey of the Commission among the twelve Member States has resulted in the following ranking of market barriers in order of importance:

(1) administrative barriers,

(2) national standards and regulations,

(3) physical frontier delays and costs,

(4) community law,

(5) restrictions in capital market,

(6) differences in VAT,

(7) regulations of freight transport,

(8) government procurement.

[Source *European Economy* (March 1988)]

There are national differences in that, for example, Italian businesspeople put government procurement second on their list, while differences in VAT was number three in importance for the French.

5.2 The benefit of the removal of barriers

The Commission has produced figures (*European Economy* no. 35 March 1988) where the benefits of the removal of trade barriers have been estimated. The theory is that it will result in a levelling of prices throughout the Community. In some countries consumers will benefit from lower prices, but the sellers of the relevant products will lose out for the same reason. In other countries consumers will have to pay more, but the sellers will gain higher profits.

The overall effect will be to reduce prices and increase employment generally. The Commission has compiled a table as a result of its studies:

	Frontier controls	Public procure-ment	Financial services	Supply effects	Total	
					Average	Range
Relative change						
As % of Gross Domestic Product (GDP)	0.4	0.5	1.5	2.1	4.5	(3.2 to 5.7)
Consumer prices	−1.0	−1.4	−1.4	−2.3	−6.1	(−4.5 to −7.7)
Absolute change						
Employment (× 1,000)	200	350	400	850	1,800	(1,300 to 2,300)
General government borrowing as a % of GDP	0.2	0.3	1.1	0.6	2.2	(1.5 to 3.0)
External balance as a % of GDP	0.2	0.1	0.3	0.4	1.0	(0.7 to 1.3)

[Source *European Economy* (March 1988)]

The Commission concluded, 'With an upturn in activity (almost 0.4% of GDP in the medium term), job creation (200,000 jobs in the medium term), disinflation (−1% of consumer price inflation in the medium term) and an easing of budgetary and external constraints (respective improvements of about 0.2 of a percentage point of GDP in the medium term), the abolition of frontier controls has the exceptional characteristic of being beneficial whatever aggregate is considered'. Although these figures were obtained from a model (or forecast) in a computer, businesses surely must agree that the abolition of these trade barriers can only be helpful.

6 | An economic check list

Those enterprises which are going to open up branches in another country, or set up an overseas sales operation, must obtain information about the relevant economic situation. Even businesses which rely on their overseas distributors or agents to report back on the market, must do their own research as part of their strategic plan as mentioned in chapter 2.

Important sources of information include:

(a) Chambers of Commerce,

(b) publications, particularly those published by the European Statistical Office,

(c) the Department of Trade and Industry or the British Overseas Board,

(d) computer data bases,

(e) professional people and organisations such as market research firms,

(f) the British Standards Institution.

Some relevant addresses are contained in Appendix 3.

APPENDIX 2
Law and the Common Market

1	**The EEC Treaty**

1.1 Background

Businesses have to work within laws, and in order to understand the effect of the Common Market, business-people should have at the least an outline knowledge of its legal basis. This is contained in the EEC Treaty, sometimes referred to as the Treaty of Rome, because representatives of the first Member States signed the document in that city on 25 March 1957.

It was the result of political thinking, which followed the devastation of the Second World War. Various European countries had cooperated together in economic projects, such as the Benelux common system of customs duties in relation to the outside world and agreed by Belgium, The Netherlands and Luxembourg. Another Treaty in 1951 established the European Coal and Steel Community between France, Germany, Italy, Belgium, The Netherlands and Luxembourg.

Countries in Europe including the United Kingdom cooperated with each other in other areas, such as the North Atlantic Treaty Organisation in defence matters, and the Council of Europe which established a Commission and a Court of Human Rights. The EEC Treaty has, however, much broader economic aims.

1.2 Summary of the EEC Treaty

The EEC Treaty is of course a long and detailed document, but the main points for businesses are as follows:

(a) The objectives of the EEC are summarised in Article 2. 'The Community shall have as its task, by establishing a common market and progressively approximating the economic policies of Member States, to promote throughout the Community a harmonious development of economic activities, a continuous and balanced expansion, an increase in stability, an accelerated raising of the standard of living and closer relations between the States belonging to it.'

(b) These objectives are to be achieved by economic means such as (1) the elimination of customs duties and of quantitive restrictions on the import and export of goods, as between members, (2) a common customs tariff, (3) a common commercial policy with other countries, (4) the abolition of obstacles to freedom of movement for persons, services and capital, also as between members, (5) a common agricultural policy, (6) a common transport policy, (7) a system ensuring the non-distortion of competition in the EEC, (8) coordination of economic policy, (9) approximation of each member's laws as needed for the proper function of the Common Market, (10) the creation of a European Social Fund for the benefit of workers, (11) the creation of a European Investment Bank, and (12) association with other countries to increase trade and to promote jointly economic and social development (Article 3).

(c) These aims are carried out through a European Parliament, a Council, a Commission and a Court of Justice (Article 4).

(d) The basis of the Community is the abolition of customs duties and similar charges between Member States (Section 1 of Chapter 1 of Title I), and the setting up of a common customs tariff against the outside world (Part 2 Section 2 Chapter 1 Title I). A Member State is not allowed to impose quantitative

restrictions in relation to goods from other Members
(Chapter 2 of Title I).

(e) Chapter 1 of Title III confirms the freedom of
movement for workers within the EEC, which is
important for those businesses in the UK sending
their employees to work in their branches elsewhere
in the EEC. Those people who provide, for example,
consultancy services within the Common Market
will be more interested in the Right of Establishment
provisions of Chapter 2. This will enable them to
establish themselves in the territories of Member
States, although there will naturally be certain
restrictions in relation to the recognition of qualifications. Lawyers from other EEC countries, for
example, will not have the same rights to practice as
they have within their national courts, because they
will not have the necessary training. Even so,
Chapter 3 provides for the ending of restrictions 'on
freedom to provide services within the Community'
(Article 59).

(f) Chapter 4 of Title III abolishes restrictions on the
movement of capital within the Community. If there
is to be more trade within the EEC it is essential that
money can be transferred freely, and some of the
newer Member States of Southern Europe will be
abolishing their own exchange control restrictions in
order to comply with this provision.

(g) The important provisions in Articles 85 and 86
relating to competition are mentioned elsewhere in 5
to 8 below, but Article 91 deals with dumping,
another means by which competition can be distorted. The practice is banned, and the Commission
may take various courses of action to deal with the
problem. Articles 92 to 94 forbid Member States
from imposing any taxation which could distort
competition within the Community by, for example,
'favouring certain undertakings or the production of
certain goods' (Article 92.1). Laws must also become

approximately the same so as to ensure fair competition (Article 100).

(h) Part 3 Title II is concerned with establishing a common economic policy. The European Currency Unit (ECU) and the European Monetary System (EMS) are both to be developed (Article 102a). An important provision for those countries which have frequent balance of payments problems. The European Commission may investigate the position and require measures to be taken to put matters right. This obviously could have an important effect on business.

(i) Title III is concerned with social provisions, and the Commission can promote cooperation between Member States in respect of employment matters, including terms of employment and 'the right of association and collective bargaining between employers and workers' (Article 118). There have been various references by English courts to the European Court of Justice to decide on the application of Article 119 to sex discrimination cases. For example, *Macarthys v Smith* [1980] ICR 672 decided that, for the purposes of deciding on what was equal pay for equal work, the men and women did not have to be contemporaneously doing equal work for the employer.

2 The European Communities Act 1972

In order to bring the Treaty of Rome into the various legal systems of the United Kingdom, Parliament had to pass the European Communities Act 1972. Section 2 of that statute also brings into effect the European Coal and Steel Community (ECSC) Treaty, and the European Atomic Energy Community (Euratom) Treaty.

This has far reaching effects, because of the way any 'rights, powers, liabilities, obligations and restrictions from time to time created or arising by or under the Treaties' can be made part of the law of the land. That can be achieved through 'Her Majesty by Order in Council' or by means of regulations made by 'a designated Minister or department'.

These regulations are usually in the form of statutory instruments, which are laid before Parliament. More fundamental changes are, however, brought in through an Act of Parliament. Part 1 of the Consumer Protection Act 1987 is an example of how our politicians gave effect to a consumer safety directive (85/374/EC) from the EEC Commission.

There are some limitations on what that Commission can do. Schedule 3 of the European Communities Act does not allow Orders in Council or regulations to make any provisions imposing or increasing taxation [para 1(a)]. This accords with the nearest document that this country has as a constitution, the Bill of Rights 1688. It declares that 'levying money for or to the use of the Crown by pretence of prerogative without consent of Parliament for longer time or in other manner than the same is or shall be granted is illegal'.

There are other important exceptions, such as regulations to take effect earlier than the time they are issued [para 1(b)], because retrospective legislation is oppressive. There are also restrictions on the creation of new criminal offences by regulation [para 1(d)].

3 | Community institutions

Although on the whole businesses will not be concerned with the procedures adopted to bringing in Community legislation, people at least should have an outline knowledge of what they are and what they do.

(a) The Commission of the EEC has seventeen members drawn from the Member States. The UK, France, Germany, Italy and Spain appoint two each, and the remaining seven countries appoint one each. Each Commissioner is in charge of one or more Directorates General, which in turn are responsible for special areas, such as competition, financial institutions and company law. With the aid of these and some specialised services the Commission formulates policy, carries out the decisions taken by the Council of Ministers, and supervises the running of Community policies. In addition to this it can take legal action against Member States which are failing to observe Community rules. This aspect of its work will be highlighted in 8 below.

(b) Most people will know about the European Parliament because of the elections that are held every five years. It is not a parliament as would be understood by the word in the UK, because in the past it has been merely consulted about proposed Community legislation. Its rule has, however, changed in that it can reject or amend the Council's proposals. If it chooses to reject what is known as the common position of the Council, then this body can only go ahead if all its members agree. If the common position is merely modified, then the Commission can review its original position, and the Council can then take various courses of action. If, for example, the Council wishes to take measures not approved by the Commission, then it has to do so unanimously. Otherwise a qualified majority will do.

(c) Mention has been made in the previous paragraph of the Council, which is made up of one representative from each of the Member States. Its function is to adopt legislation for the Community, so in this sense it is like what in the UK would be called Parliament. It is, however, not elected, but each Member State's government makes the appointments.

(d) The Court of Justice has played an important part in harmonising Community law, and some of its decisions are noted in 8 below. Each Member State appoints a judge, and the institution has been so successful that a Court of First Instance is likely to be formed. In theory this should ease the workload, although there is a danger that this will merely make legal actions more lengthy, in that there will now be an appeals procedure. At present the Court hears cases against Community Institutions and Member States. It also hears appeals from the highest Appeal Courts of each Member States, if they involve questions of Community law. Such questions may be referred to it by national courts.

(e) The Court of Auditors checks the Community's revenue and expenditure.

(f) The European Investment Bank lends money for Community projects.

(g) Another consultative body, this time in relation to economic and social matters, is the Economic and Social Council of 156 members consisting of representatives from employers and consumer organisations and Trade Unions.

4	## The Single European Act

Any relationship tends to change with the passing years, and the countries of the European Community decided to modify the various Treaties, so that this would be reflected. This resulted in the Single European Act, another Treaty, which was signed in 1986.

Although it affects the economy of the various countries, and is therefore important for business, there are hints of a wider purpose. The preamble refers to transforming relations among the various Member States into a European Union in accordance with the Solemn Declaration of Stuttgart of 19 June 1983. This will be achieved by, among other things, 'European Cooperation among the Signatory States in the sphere of foreign policy'. Such statements emphasise that some politicians would like to see closer political relations, and prompted a debate in October 1988 when the UK Prime Minister, Mrs Thatcher opposed such ideas.

There is, however, a political dimension, which prompted a Polish writer, the late Aleksander Bregman, to summarise an important achievement in the sphere of European unity: 'Even if there have been setbacks in recent years, the accomplishment has been a fundamental element of change for the better' (*Zakamarki Historii – The Crannies of History* – Polska Fundacja Kulturalna 1968 London at page 15).

Despite these political undertones the Single European Act has also introduced the idea of 31 December 1992 as the date by which 'The internal market shall comprise an area without internal frontiers in which the free movement of goods, persons, services and capital is ensured in accordance with the provisions of this Treaty' [now Article 8a of the EEC Treaty].

The European Commission, in drawing up its proposals to achieve the objectives, must take into account the different stage of development of the various economies [Article 8b]. Now that the Common Market has many more Member States, this is obviously a necessary proviso.

The decision-making power in some areas, such as policies in relation to the movement of capital, is in the Council of Ministers who can issue directives as a result of recommendations from the Commission 'acting by a qualified majority'. They only need to come to unanimous decisions where they are, for example, adopting measures 'which constitute a step back as regards the liberalisation of capital movements' [the new Article 70(a) of the EEC Treaty].

The Council of Ministers also has to remove obstacles to a Single European Market by ensuring that certain national laws of Member States approximate to each other in accordance with Article 100 of the Treaty. The Single European Act emphasises this by adding a new Article 100a, which also requires the Council to act by a qualified majority in this area. They do this as a result of a recommendation from the Commission in cooperation with the European Parliament, but also have the duty to consult the Economic and Social Committee. By Article 100a a high level of emphasis is to be afforded to health, safety, environmental and consumer protection.

Similar qualified majorities are required in the fields

of social policy such as the harmonisation of conditions in the working environment [Article 118a], but any measures to be taken have to avoid any constraints with the effect of holding back the creation and development of small and medium-sized undertakings [Article 118a(2)]. As part of its work here the Commission has to try to develop dialogue between management and labour at European level [Article 118b].

The Council, however, has to act unanimously on a proposal from the Commission in relation to proposed harmonisation of legislation concerning various types of taxation. It also has to consult the European Parliament in this respect.

Taxation of course has an important effect on the economy and businesses, but there are also other aspects of the Single European Act which could affect them more directly, for example:

(a) There is a greater emphasis on cooperation in economic and monetary union, and the Member States are urged to take account of the experience 'acquired in cooperation within the framework of the European Monetary System (EMS) and in developing the ECU . . .'. The ECU is the European Currency Unit, and is already used by some European multinational companies for internal accounting between their various branches and associate companies. As far as banks are concerned, it is just a currency like any other. The United Kingdom, however, has not joined the EMS, a system designed to ensure that the currencies of the participants do not fluctuate too much in relation to each other.

(b) A potentially useful provision for businesses is found in Article 130(a), where the Community has to reduce 'disparities between the various regions and the backwardness of the least-favoured regions'. The intention is to encourage the various facilities such as the European Agricultural Guidance and Guarantee Fund, the Guidance Section, the European Social

Fund and the European Regional Development Fund. Indeed, the latter fund has already provided funds in the UK as its purposes are to participate 'in the development and structural adjustment of regions whose development is lagging behind and in the conversion of declining industrial regions'. This has opened up a source of funds for those businesses in declining areas in the UK, e.g. shipbuilding towns, who need consultancy services in order to run their enterprises more efficiently and to expand. (c) Those industries who rely on research and development can benefit from a new Title VI to Part 3 of the Treaty. The Community is to promote cooperation among research establishments and 'undertakings'. Money is of course available to assist in these projects such as the Framework programme. Information technology receives assistance under the ESPRIT scheme, while there is a more general programme called EUREKA of which the European Commission is a member. Addresses are contained Appendix 3.

There are some minor qualifications by certain countries to the Single European Act. Greece, for example, has declared in an annex to the Act that Community policies and measures in relation to currency exchange and rail, road and inland water transport should not harm sensitive sectors of Member States' economies. Portugal made similar comments about such transport as well as the freedom of the nationals of Member States to provide services in the Community. Ireland is concerned about its insurance industry, and has requested sympathetic treatment if its government feels that special provisions in this respect have to be made.

All these reservations mean that there may be problems ahead, when new measures are proposed to implement the Single Market. Exceptions may be made for certain countries, so enterprises seeking to do business abroad will have to check the rules as well as all the other aspects in creating the business plan.

5 Some sources of Community law

5.1 Regulations

These are made by the Council or Commission and are directly applicable throughout the Community, but they must be made in accordance with the Treaty and published in the Official Journal. For example, Council Regulation 1975/69 and Commission Regulation 2195/69 provided for the payment of a premium in respect of slaughtered dairy cows.

5.2 Directives

Directives are made by the Council or Commission and are addressed to States.

5.3 Decisions

A decision by the Council or Commission is binding on those to whom it is addressed.

5.4 The Court

The court, as illustrated by the cases mentioned in 8 below, has a great influence on the interpretation of Community law. The Treaties merely contain statements of principle unlike Acts of Parliament in the UK, which usually contain detailed provisions. There are signs of change in that, for example, the Data Protection Act 1984, contains the text of the Council of Europe Convention for the Protection of Individuals with Regard to Automatic Processing of Personal Data. That Act, however, contains detailed definitions in the UK fashion as to registration and enforcement.

6 Article 85 and competition

Some large companies or groups of businesses may wish to control competition in order to maintain their market share. They could, for example, agree to sell to distributors only in specific areas. Examples of such practices are noted in 8 below.

Article 85 therefore prohibits various practices such as the fixing of prices and other contractual terms, the limitation or control of production, markets, technical development, or investment, the sharing of markets or sources of supply. An overriding principle is the banned agreements or contractual terms which affect trade between member states. They must also have the object or effect of restricting or distorting competition within the Common Market. The effects of Article 85 on the appointments of agents and distributors are set out in chapter 3.

7 Article 86 and abuse of a dominant position

Some businesses are of course very large, and they could use their dominant positions to stifle any competition. If they then become monopolies, they can then charge what they like for their goods and services, which is contrary to the spirit of the Treaty, e.g. 'the institution of a system ensuring that competition in the common market is not distorted' [Article 3(f)].

Article 86 therefore prohibits the abuse of a dominant position within the Common Market or a substantial part of it provided that it affects trade between Member States. Examples include the imposition of unfair trading conditions, or the limitation of production, markets, or technical development to the prejudice of consumers. This latter word is not defined, so it could have a much wider meaning than that given to it in the laws of the UK, such as the Consumer Protection Act 1987. It could therefore include not just the general public but business consumers. How the courts have dealt with competition in general is noted in 8 below.

8 Unfair competition and the courts

Because the rules against unfair competition are so important, there have been a lot of cases before the

European and national courts. They provide some useful guidance to businesses, both to comply with the law or where they are adversely affected by a breach of it. Some of the more important decisions are set out below.

(1) *Garden Cottage Foods Ltd v Milk Marketing Board* [1984] AC 130. This was a House of Lords case about the refusal by the Milk Marketing Board to sell to more than four distributors in England and Wales. Garden Cottage would probably have been forced out of business, so the law lords were prepared to grant damages for a breach of Article 86.

(2) *GEC/Weir Sodium Circulators* 1977 OJ L327/26. The Commission considered a joint venture for the joint development, production and sale of sodium circulators. It decided that if the parent companies, as part of the contract, had agreed to cooperate in certain activities through that joint venture, this would restrict competition in contravention of Article 85.

(3) *Pilkington/BSN-Gervais Danone* 1980 reported in the Commission's *Tenth Report on Competition Policy*. Pilkington's plan to buy a French glass company's subsidiaries threatened to be an abuse of its domination of the flat glass market in Europe. The Commission therefore sent out a warning, and the purchase was limited to a German company. Restrictions were agreed on the planned cooperation between the French and UK companies. Note that share acquisitions may fall within Article 85 (Philip Morris 1987 case 142/84). This can happen where the investor has obtained legal or actual control of the other's 'commercial conduct'. Another instance is where there is a cooperation agreement between the investor and the other party. Option agreements allowing the investor to take control at a later stage are also banned, and so is any shareholder agreement where the company and the investor are going to cooperate with each other.

(4) *Pronuptia de Paris GmbH, Frankfurt am Main v Schillgalis* [1986] *The Times* 6 February 1986. Franchising agreements must not contain restrictive clauses to contravene Article 85.

(5) *Bureau National Interprofessionel Du Cognac v Clair* [1985] Case 123/83. A trade association which fixed minimum prices for cognac did so in breach of Article 85.

(6) The Commission has issued a notice [OJ 1986 C231] by which it has defined the meaning of 'substantial' in Articles 85 and 86. The aggregate turnover of the participating undertakings must not exceed 200 million ECU in the previous financial year excluding dealings between the participants. Market share is that the goods or services supplied by the participant do not represent more than 5% of the product market in the area of Common Market affected. An increase in relation to market share and turnover for not more than two successive financial years is to be ignored.

(7) *Demo-Studio Schmidt v Commission* [1984] 1 CMLR 63. In accordance with the manufacturer's policy a retailer, whose business was open for limited hours, was not appointed a distributor of certain hi-fi equipment. The criteria for such an appointment required him among others to remain open at certain times, but this did not contravene Article 85.

(8) In *Commission v Ireland* [1982] ECR 4005 a government sponsored 'buy Irish' campaign was intended to persuade people to buy nationally pro-duced goods instead of imported goods and therefore was liable to affect trade between Member States in contravention of Article 30 of the Treaty.

(9) *Johnson & Johnson* OJ 1980 L377/16. A German company found it cheaper to buy from a British wholesaler, whose agreement with its own supplier forbade it to export goods. Johnson & Johnson should

have known that this was wrong, and should have prevented its subsidiaries from adopting such a policy.

(10) *Comptoir Français de l'Azote* [1968] CMLR D57. Three producers of compound fertiliser were fined for selling to Germany through a single jointly-owned distributor.

(11) *Rennet* [1980] 2 CMLR 402. Exclusive purchasing agreements are contrary to Article 86 of the Treaty.

(12) *Davidson Rubber* [1972] CMLR D52. An exclusive patent agreement is not contrary to Article 85.

(13) Although tied house agreements are contrary to Article 85, there is a block exemption in relation to beer under the Commission Regulation 194/83. The purchaser of the beer must not be prevented from buying other goods and services from other suppliers.

(14) *Windsurfer Case* 193/83. The licensor of a patent is not allowed to approve all similar products of the licensee or impose conditions not essential for the exploitation of the product.

| 9 | ## Doing business in Europe legally |

Lawyers therefore play an important part in a European expansion plan. They can, for example, draft agreements which comply with Community law. Many smaller firms, however, will not have the expertise in this area, although the Law Society is encouraging them to participate in courses. The Society can also provide information about those solicitors, which specialise in Community matters.

APPENDIX 3
Useful names and addresses

British embassies

Britannia House
Rue Joseph II 28
1040 Brussels
Belgium
Tel: Brussels 2179000

36–40 Kastelsvej
DK 2100
Copenhagen
Denmark
Tel: Copenhagen 26 4600

35 Rue de Fauberg St
  Honoré
75383 Paris
France
Tel: Paris 42 66 9142
There is also representation
at Bordeaux, Lille, Lyons
and Marseilles

Friedrich-Ebert Allee 77
5300 Bonn 1
Germany
Tel: Bonn 234 061
There is also representation
at Berlin, Düsseldorf,
Frankfurt, Hamburg,
Munich and Stuttgart

1 Ploutarchou St
Athens
GR 10675
Greece
Tel: Athens 72362 11

33 Merrion Road
Dublin 4
Ireland
Tel: Dublin 695211

Via XX Settembre 80A
00187 Rome
Italy
Tel: Rome 4755441 and
  4755551

The main commercial post
and central point for
British trade in Italy is
British Consulate-General
Via San Paolo 7
20121 Milan
Italy
Tel: Milan 863442
There is also representation
in Naples, Turin, Cagliari
and Venice

14 Boulevard Roosevelt
L-2449
Luxembourg Ville
Luxembourg
Tel: Luxembourg 29864

Lange Voorhout 10
2514 ED
The Hague
The Netherlands
Tel: The Hague 645800

35–37 Rua de S Domingos
a Lapa 1296
Lisbon
Portugal
Tel: Lisbon 6611915,
661147, 663181 and
661122
There is also representation
at Oporto

Calle de Ferndando el
Santo 16
Madrid 28010
Spain
Tel: Madrid 419-200
There is also representation
at Barcelona, Bilbao and
Las Palmas

Chambers of commerce

Britanny Chamber of
Commerce
Chambre Régionale de
Commerce et D'Industrie
de Bretagne
69 Cannon Street
London
EC4N 5AB
Tel: 01-329 4083
Tx: 88941 Attn CRCIB
Fax: 01-329 4137
This Chamber of
Commerce is looking for
UK outlets of Breton
products

German Chamber of
Industry and Commerce
12–13 Suffolk Street
St James's
London
SW1Y 4HG
Tel: 01-930 7251
Tx: 919442 GERMAN G
Fax: 01-930 2726
This Chamber of
Commerce is looking for
UK outlets of German
products

Italian Chamber of
Commerce for Great
Britain
Walmar House
296 Regent Street
London
W1R 6AE
Tel: 01-637 3153
Tx: 269096 ITACAM
Fax: 01-436 6037

The Netherlands–British
Chamber of Commerce
The Dutch House
307–308 High Holborn
London
WC1V 7LS
Tel: 01-505 1358
Tx: 23211

Scottish Life House
48 St Vincent Street
Glasgow
G2 5TS
Tel: 041-2211331

41 Spring Gardens
Manchester
M2 2BB
Tel: 061-8345674
Tx: 669489 MPS G
This Chamber of
Commerce publishes
useful books and bulletins
of use to businesses
wishing to do business in
The Netherlands. There are
two other addresses of use
to enterprises wishing to

know more about agents
and franchising in that
country

Agents:
Nederlands Verbond van
Tussenpersonen
Postbus 19352
1000 GJ Amsterdam
The Netherlands
Tel: Amsterdam 221944
Tx: 18313

Franchising:
Nederlandse Franchising
Verenging
Arubalaan
1213 VG Hilversum
The Netherlands
Tel: Amsterdam 833934

Spanish Chamber of
Commerce in Great
Britain
5 Cavendish Square
London
W1M 0DP
Tel: 01-637 9061
Tx: 8811583 CAMCOE G
Fax: 01-436 7188
More particular advice can
be obtained from the
British Chambers of
Commerce in Spain, whose
addresses are:
Plaza Sta. Bárbara, 10
28004 Madrid
Spain
Tel: Madrid 410 70 64
Tx: 45522 CCBE E

1º Pasea de Gracia, 11
08007 Barcelona
Spain
Tel: Barcelona 317 32 20
Tx: 516891 BCOM E

Alameda de Mazarredo, 5
48001 Bilbao
Spain
Tel: Bilbao 423 86 05
Tx: 31276

Portuguese Chamber of
    Commerce & Industry
    in the UK
4th Floor
New Bond Street House
1–5 New Bond Street
London
W1Y 9PE
Tel: 01-493 9973
Tx: 918089
Fax: 01-493 4772

London Chamber of
Commerce
69 Cannon Street
London
EC4N 5AB
Tel: 01-248 4444
Local Chambers of
Commerce are also very
helpful

Confederation of British Industry

CBI Initiative 1992
Centre Point
103 New Oxford Street
London
WC1A 1DU
Tel: 01-836 1992

Design

Design Council
28 Haymarket
London
SW1Y 4SU
Tel: 01-839 8000
This provides a design
advisory service to
industry, but the British
Standards Institution (see
General Advice below) may
be helpful concerning
technical aspects

Exporting

Exports to Europe Branch
The Department of Trade
and Industry
1–19 Victoria Street
London
SW1H 0ET
Tel: 01-215 5486 Belgium
and Luxembourg
01-215 5140 Denmark
01-215 4762 France
01-215 4776 Greece
01-215 4783 Ireland
01-215 5103 Italy
01-215 5549 Multi-country
01-215 4790 The
Netherlands
01-215 5307 Portugal
01-215 4260 Spain
01-215 4796 West Germany
The DTI has various
regional offices as noted in
the telephone directory

British Exporters
Association
16 Dartmouth Street
London
SW1H 9BL
Tel: 01-222 5419
The British Standards
Institution (see General
Advice below) also offers
technical help to exporters

Export Credits Guarantee

PO Box 272
Aldermanbury House
Aldermanbury
London
EC2P 2EL
Tel: 01-382 7000

Fleming House
134 Renfrew Street
Glasgow
G3 6TL
Tel: 041-332 8707

Crown Building
Cathays Park
Cardiff
CF1 3NH
Tel: (0222) 824100

12th Floor
Windsor House
9–15 Bedford Street
Belfast
BT2 7EG
Tel: (0232) 231743
There are also regional
offices throughout England

General advice

The Department of Trade &
  Industry
1–19 Victoria Street
London
SW1H 0ET
Tel: 01-215 7877

Welsh Office Industry
  Department
New Crown Building
Cathays Park
Cardiff
CF1 3NQ
Tel: (0222) 825097

Confederation of British
  Industry
Centre Point
103 New Oxford Street
London
WC1A 1DU
Tel: 01-379 7400

Scottish Export Office
Industry Department for
  Scotland
Alhambra House
45 Waterloo Street
Glasgow
G2 6AT
Tel: 041-248 2855

Industrial Development
  Board for Northern
  Ireland
IDB House
64 Chichester Street
Belfast
BT1 4JX
Tel: (0232) 233233

The British Standards
  Institution
2 Park Street
London
W1A 2BS
Tel: 01-629 9000
Tx: 266933 BSILON G
Fax: 01-629 0506

Grants and sources of funds

World Aid Section
Room 042
Department of Trade and
  Industry
1–19 Victoria Street
London
SW1H 0ET
Tel: 01-215 4279

European Social Fund
Department of
  Employment
St Vincent House
30 Orange Street
London
WC2H 7HT
Tel: 01-930 5597
  01-930 8698

European Regional
  Development Fund
Investment, Development
  and Accountancy
  Division
Department of Trade and
  Industry
Room 229
66–74 Victoria Street
London
SW1E 6SW
Tel: 01-215 2556

Importing

British Importers Confederation
69 Cannon Street
London
EC4N 5AB
Tel: 01-248 4444
Tx: 888941 LCCI G

Languages

Institute of Linguists 24a Highbury Grove London N5 2EA Tel: 01-359 7445	Institute of Translators & Interpreting 318a Finchley Road London NW5 5AT Tel: 01-794 9931

Centre for Information on
  Language Teaching &
  Research
Regents College
Inner Circle
Regents Park
London
NW1 4NS
Tel: 01-486 8221
	Language Advisory &
	  Referral Service
	London Chamber of
	  Commerce
	69 Cannon Street
	London
	EC4N 5AB
	Tel: 01-248 4444 ext 2077
	  or 2076

Law

The Law Society
Law Society's Hall
113 Chancery Lane
London
WC2
Tel: 01-242 1222

Marketing

British Overseas Trade Board Fairs & Promotions Branch Dean Bradley House 52 Horseferry Road London SW1P 2AG Tel: 01-212 7676 Tx: 297121	Institute of Marketing Moor Hall Cookham Maidenhead Berks SL6 9QH Tel: (062 85) 24922 (Courses on marketing)

Market research

The Statistical Office of
  the European
  Communities
Eurostat
Directorate A
L-2920
Luxembourg
Tel: 4301 4567

Central Office of
  Information
(Overseas Publicity
  Services)
Hercules Road
London
SE1 7DU
Tel: 01-928 2345

Market Research Society
15 Belgrave Square
London
SW1X 8PE
Tel: 01-235 4709

British Overseas Trade
  Board
Statistics & Market
  Intelligence Library
1–19 Victoria Street
London
SW1H 0ET
Tel: 01-215 5444
Tx: 881074

Business Statistics Office
Cardiff Road
Newport
Gwent
NP9 1XG
Tel: (0633) 56111

Public purchasing

Details of certain European Community public works and
supplies contracts are published in the daily supplement to
the *Official Journal of the European Communities*,
obtainable from:
HMSO
Publications Centre
PO Box 276
London
SW8 5DR
Tel: 01-622 3316
Tx: 297138

Purchasing and supply

The Institute of Purchasing
  and Supply
Easton House
Easton on the Hill
Stamford
Lincolnshire
PE9 3NZ
Tel: (0780) 56777

Research and development

The UK EUREKA Office
Department of Trade and
  Industry
Room 204
Ashdown House
123 Victoria Street
London
SW1E 6RB
Chambers of Commerce
can also be very helpful,
while another possible
source of information is the
British Standards
Institution noted under
General Advice above

Small businesses

Association of
  Independent Businesses
Trowbray House
108 Weston Street
London
SE1 3QB
Tel: 01-403 4066

Council for Small
  Businesses in Rural
  Areas
141 Castle Street
Salisbury
Wiltshire
SP1 3TP
Tel: (0722) 336255

Local Enterprise
  Development Unit
Ledu House
Upper Galwally
Belfast
BT8 4TB
Tel: (0232) 691031

Scottish Development
  Agency
Small Business Division
Rosebery House
Haymarket Terrace
Edinburgh
EH12 5EZ
Tel: 031-337 9595

Welsh Development
  Agency
Small Business Unit
Treforest Industrial Estate
Pontypridd
Mid Glamorgan
CF37 5UT
Tel: (044 385) 2666

Technical standards

British Standards Institution
2 Park Street
London
W1A 2BS
Tel: 01-629 9000
Tx: 266933 BSILON G
Fax: 01-629 0506

APPENDIX 4
Bibliography

Business strategy

The Business Plan Workbook · *Authors* Colin and Paul Barrow · *Publisher* Kogan Page 1988
This is a very useful outline of how a business plan is built up, and it contains some useful sections on market research and the operations plan.

Business Strategy · *Editor* H. Igor Ansoff · *Publisher* Penguin Books 1983

Corporate Planning in Practice · *Authors* John Fawn and Bernard Cox · *Publisher* Kogan Page 1987

Competitive Advantage · *Author* Michael E. Porter *Publisher* Free Press (New York) 1985

Credit control

Management of Trade Credit 3rd Edition · *Authors* Thomas Guybon Hutson and John Butterworth · *Publisher* Gower Publishing Company Limited 1984

Economics

Some useful books as introductions to the economy of the European Community are:

Europe in Figures · Office for Official Publications of the European Communities 1987

The Economics of the Common Market 6th edition · *Author* Dennis Swann · *Publisher* Penguin Books 1988

Europe's Domestic Market · *Authors* Jacques Pelkmans and Alan Winters · *Publisher* Routledge (for the Royal Institute of Affairs) 1988

The Logic of Unity – A Geography of the European Economic Community 3rd edition · *Author* Geoffrey Parker · *Publisher* Longman Group Limited 1981
This particular edition does not include the changes introduced by the addition of Spain, Greece and Portugal to the Community, but it contains useful information about the remaining countries.

The New Europe – An Economic Geography of the EEC 3rd edition · *Author* G. N. Minshull · *Publisher* Hodder & Stoughton Educational 1988

The European Challenge 1992 – The Benefits of a Single Market · *Author* Paolo Cecchini · *Publisher* Wildwood House Limited 1988
This is a summary of the believed economic benefits of the removal of the remaining trade barriers, and is the result of research sponsored by the Commission of the European Communities. More detailed statistics will be found in:

The European Economy No 35 – The Economics of 1992 · Directorate General for Economic and Financial Affairs Commission of the European Communities March 1988

The Statistical Office of the European Communities publishes various books on statistics relating to economics such as:

The Basic Statistics of the Community
Demographic Statistics
Social Indicators for the EC
Employment and Unemployment
Labour Force Survey
Money and Finance
Industry (Statistical Yearbook)
Short-term Trends
Structure and Activity of Industry
Industrial Production (quarterly)
Carriage of Goods
Balance of Payments

Exporting

Hints to exporters in respect of specific countries which are published by the British Overseas Trade Board provide useful introductions

Financial analysis

Managerial Finance · *Authors* J. Fred Weston and Thomas E. Copeland · *Publisher* HRW International Edition 1986

Management of Company Finance · *Authors* J. M. Samuels and F. M. Wilkes · *Publisher* Van Nostrand Reinhold (UK) Co Ltd 1986

Languages

The Register of Translators & Translating Agencies · *Editors* Phillip Morris and Geoff Weston · *Publisher* Merton Press

Law

Consumer Protection Act 1987: A practical guide · *Author* Peter M. Walker · *Publisher* Longman Professional 1987

Forms and Agreements on Intellectual Property and International Licensing 3rd Edition · *Author* L. W. Melville · *Publisher* Sweet & Maxwell Limited 1979 revised 1988

Law and Institutions of the European Community 4th edition · *Authors* D. Lasok and J. W. Bridge · *Publisher* Butterworths 1987

INDEX